Kenneth

SIX STEPS *to* EXCELLENCE IN MINISTRY

KENNETH
COPELAND
PUBLICATIONS

Six Steps to Excellence in Ministry
Study Guide

ISBN 1-57562-783-3   30-0736

09 08 07 06 05 04   6 5 4 3 2 1

Kenneth Copeland Publications
Fort Worth, Texas 76192-0001

For more information about Kenneth Copeland Ministries, call 1-800-600-7395 or visit www.kcm.org.

1

"According to the glorious gospel of the blessed God, which was committed to my trust. And I thank Christ Jesus our Lord, who hath enabled me, for that he counted me faithful, putting me into the ministry."

1 Timothy 1:11-12

A ministry of excellence will pay whatever price is necessary to get the job done and done God's way.

> # TAPE/CD ONE
> ## God's Power Through You—A Vessel of Honor

"For I am not ashamed of the gospel of Christ: for it is the power of God unto salvation to every one that believeth."
Romans 1:16

A ministry of excellence absolutely will not tolerate unbelief in itself. It will not tolerate taking the easy way.

Expect Excellence

FOCUS: "That ye might walk worthy of the Lord unto all pleasing, being fruitful in every good work, and increasing in the knowledge of God" (Colossians 1:10).

Believers demand excellence from God and have every right to expect the very best from Him. He, Himself, has set the standard of excellence for the Body of Christ. He is the ultimate example of complete success. In the same way, you should be ready, willing and dedicated to demand excellence from yourself.

The same holds true in a ministry. If you are a pastor, you are required by God to demand excellence out of your congregation as well as those who work with you in your ministry. As a minister called out into the field, you will demand excellence from the people who work for you and from the congregations you serve. You must be willing to demand the highest form of excellence from the ministries you are involved in.

> *You should be ready, willing and dedicated to demand excellence from yourself.*

The Apostle Paul recognized the gravity of his calling. He knew that the gospel was committed into his trust. "According to the glorious gospel of the blessed God, which was committed to my trust" (1 Timothy 1:11). Paul took the training of his disciples very seriously because he realized they were handling the mightiest power in the universe. He wrote, "For I am not ashamed of the gospel of Christ: for it is the power of God unto salvation to every one that believeth" (Romans 1:16). The gospel is the power of God! The gospel is not only the power by which a person is saved from hell, it is also God's unlimited ability so save, heal and deliver.

As a minister of the gospel, you are entrusted with God's strength and might. You are therefore faced with two responsibilities: 1) to develop and maintain excellence of ministry and 2) to deal with Satan.

Excellence in ministry absolutely will not tolerate unbelief, failure or taking the easy way out. A ministry of excellence will pay whatever price is necessary to get the job done and done right—God's way, based on His Word. This way Jesus will be represented well. Your ministry represents Jesus Christ to the world. Yours is a sacred calling. It must be executed with dedication and integrity. You are expected to demonstrate absolute honesty and commitment. Without a firm decision to succeed with God's help, you cannot hope to maintain the measure of maturity and perfection that your ministry must command.

Having acknowledged the call and anointing of God upon your life, you pose a serious threat to Satan. In his eyes, you have become the most dangerous living thing on this globe. Your second responsibility is to contend with him.

Satan is not worried about God. He is postponing that inevitable confrontation as long as he can. But since you represent God's divine power and authority in this world, the adversary *must* reckon with *you*. If you were to die now, the devil would not care whether you went to heaven or hell. Either way, you would be forever removed from the field of battle and out of his way. What Satan *does* fear is a person who is born again—one who has God's divine nature in his spirit. Only such a person can wield the sword of the Spirit— the Word of God—with accuracy. You are dangerous to him, and you *will* have to resist him.

When you strap on the full armor of God (Ephesians 6:11), you must be prepared and determined to use it. The evil one will certainly attack you with all the forces of darkness. But at the same time, be prepared for victory! *All the combined forces of hell are not powerful enough to defeat you!*

The armory of the devil and of his cohorts is restricted to that which is common to man (1 Corinthians 10:13). He cannot go back into his knowledge of spiritual warfare and make use of supernatural weaponry. His power and his arms are limited! Satan has no secret tactics to call upon to prevail against you if you will but stand firm. The God-given weapons of your warfare are mighty through God to the pulling down of strongholds (2 Corinthians 10:4). Satan is limited. You are not. The victory is yours! First John 4:4 and 1 Corinthians 15:57 guarantee it. "...Greater is he that is in you, than he that is in the world."

"Thanks be to God, which giveth us the victory through our Lord Jesus Christ." ❧

Dedication Is Your Decision

FOCUS: "In a great house there are not only vessels of gold and of silver, but also of wood and of earth; and some to honour, and some to dishonour. If a man therefore purge himself from these, he shall be a vessel unto honour, sanctified, and meet for the master's use, and prepared unto every good work" (2 Timothy 2:20-21).

The first step to excellence in ministry and the key to receiving God's power is *dedication.* Make the quality decision—a decision that with God's help you will never violate, never turn back from—to have a ministry of excellence. Men will not be able to change you, circumstances will not be able to change you, a matter of life and death will not change you and feelings will have no bearing on your commitment.

> *The first step to excellence in ministry and the key to receiving God's power is dedication.*

True dedication simply makes a decision based on one's commitment to God. For example, many people pray and beg God to give them a burden for souls, an overwhelming feeling that will *make* them win the lost. Such praying is foolish in light of the teachings of the New Testament. Nowhere are you told to pray this way. You are, however, commanded by Jesus Christ Himself to, "Go ye into all the world, and preach the gospel to every creature" (Mark 16:15). The very fact that a person prays for a burden is evidence that he already has a heart to win souls. All he has to do is obey the commandment. If Jesus told you to do it, that should be sufficient motivation whether you feel like it or not.

The Bible says that Jesus was moved with compassion. What is compassion? It is love. God is love. Therefore, compassion is a person. If Compassion told you to go, then you should be moved by Compassion and pursue the task. You should be moved by what God has said, not by feelings.

Just as a marriage union is solidified by a commitment of faith instead of emotions, the stability of your ministry does not depend on your feelings. A decision for a ministry of excellence then, is a deep, firm resolution.

True commitment can also be compared to a pilot in a single-engine airplane. If the engine fails in midair, the pilot is committed to landing his craft. He has no choice. His feelings of fear, doubt or inadequacy are of absolutely no consequence. He will land his plane one way or another. If he has committed himself to flying, he will take control and land the best he can to spare his life and the lives of his passengers.

As you accept the call to ministry, you face this kind of commitment. How you handle it now could determine whether you succeed or fail and even whether you live or die. Take the time to get before God, and get in the Word. Stay there and rest in the Lord until the Holy Spirit and the Word of God do something to your willingness to be committed. Without a firm decision, Satan will take advantage of every opportunity to make your life a failure. But Philippians 2:13 says that God is at work in you both to will and to do of His good pleasure. He is faithful, and He will create in you the power and the desire to make an uncompromised decision.

When you finally make a full, no quit, no turning back, forever commitment to God, fulfilling your calling will be the most exciting thing you've ever done.

Don't be afraid to accept the responsibility of making the decision. God has provided the power, furnished the weapons and equipped you with everything you need. It is the same as experiencing the new birth. Once you made the decision, God did the rest. His power, His Spirit and His Word performed their functions, and you were born again. A decision was all it took. Your part is to determine in your heart to obey your calling, and then God will do His part.

Never be deceived into thinking that being in the will of God is expensive. The most costly thing on this planet is being out of the will of God. You cannot afford it. ◅◌▻

Find Your Place

FOCUS: "And he gave some, apostles; and some, prophets; and some, evangelists; and some, pastors and teachers; for the perfecting of the saints, for the work of the ministry..." (Ephesians 4:11-12).

The Bible says that the callings of God are without repentance (Romans 11:29). If you are called to be an apostle, prophet, evangelist, pastor, teacher or to any other ministry in the Body of Christ, the Lord will not revoke your assignment. He ordained you before the foundation of the world. When you stand before the judgment seat of Christ, it will be in the light of your calling—not what you did, nor what you meant to do or wished you had done, but what God said you were appointed to do. Whether you fulfill your call or not is your decision. This applies not only to the fivefold ministry but to every member of Christ's Body.

> *Each believer is anointed and endued with power to fulfill a specific function.*

Each believer is anointed and endued with power to fulfill a specific function. By the Spirit of God, every individual is able to perform their calling with mastery and excellence. So it would be to your advantage to find your calling and get in it!

You may have to change your thinking to find your place. If you have some unscriptural religious traditions, you will have to discard them. For example, 2 Timothy 2:20 says, "But in a great house there are not only vessels of gold and of silver, but also of wood and of earth; and some to honour, and some to dishonour." Many who read or preach this verse, stop right there and say, "Not everyone can have the kind of excellent ministry someone like Brother Copeland has because in a great house there are some vessels to honor and some to dishonor. Some are vessels of gold, but some are required to be earthen vessels."

This is nonsense! Satan will attempt to twist the Scriptures to keep people bowed down and trying to please God based on their feeling and false humility. The hypocrisy of this thinking is clearly seen when the same people become angry if someone tells them how worthless, unworthy and no good they or their children are. They would go to court over that. Yet the same people tell God these very things about themselves and call it humility.

Verse 21 continues: "If a man therefore purge himself from these, he shall be a vessel unto honour, sanctified, and meet for the master's use, and prepared unto every good work." *Meet* is an Old English word that means "able." It is important to God the Father that you be a vessel unto honor, yielded to His Word to do His will here in the earth.

> It is important to God the father that you be a vessel unto honor.

Whether you become a gold vessel or a mud pot is not the Master's decision—it's yours.

Have you ever watched a master craftsman at his trade? How does he treat his tools? He is not negligent and careless. His tools are specially designed and tempered, full of strength and power to do specific tasks. As a skilled craftsman, he depends on his instruments for his livelihood. He meticulously uses, cares for and maintains the tools of his trade. They are extensions of his creativity. He intends for them to last a lifetime and that they be handed down to his son after him. The tools of a man's trade take care of him, and he takes care of them.

In the redemption of the human race, you are the tool of God's craft. Jesus is the Redeemer, but you are the bearer of the good news. He is the vine, but you are the branch that bears the fruit. He will care for you and sustain you. He will temper you. A wrench is not tempered by beating it over an anvil. People have the mistaken idea that to strengthen a believer God has to beat and harass him.

No! It takes oil to temper steel. The oil of the Holy Spirit toughens and reinforces you. Your strength and power lie in the Word of God and His Spirit indwelling you. ◁⑨

Devote Yourself to Pleasing God

FOCUS: "And he that sent me is with me: the Father hath not left me alone; for I do always those things that please him" (John 8:29).

A decision for total dedication includes a determination to please God. Go through the New Testament and learn those things that bring Him pleasure. For instance, Hebrews 11:6 says, "But without faith it is impossible to please him." You must walk by faith to please God.

The Father is not delighted when you are walking in the flesh—or are carnally minded. You must be spiritually minded (Romans 8:1-8).

God receives no enjoyment from your defeat. He was grieved with the children of Israel because they were overcome in the wilderness. "For some, when they had heard, did provoke: howbeit not all that came out of Egypt by Moses. But with whom was he grieved forty years? was it not with them that had sinned, whose carcases fell in the wilderness?" (Hebrews 3:16-17). When you do not walk in victory is just as offensive to Him.

The decision to please the Father must include the decision to live in victory. The victory that overcomes the world is faith (1 John 5:4). God intends that you use your faith for every endeavor in life because Romans 1:17 says, "The just shall live by faith."

You must also live and walk in the love of God. Getting strife out of your life is part of your dedication to God. This requires a firm, quality decision of the highest order. Strife should be avoided and stopped at all costs. It is playing the devil's game and he always wins in an atmosphere where there is disharmony.

Brother Copeland demands excellence from his staff, yet is supportive of a person who is falling short of perfection in his work. Because of his commitment to walk in the love of God, he stays with the person and stands by him as long as he makes every effort to succeed. He works with the person to see that the accuracy and perfection they are capable of is attained with God's help.

But one thing that is not tolerated from Brother Copeland's staff is a person who causes strife because it is so destructive.

Avoiding strife is not a suggestion. It is a command. Look again at 2 Timothy 2:21, "If a man therefore purge himself from these...." What are the "these" to which Paul refers? Verses 22-24 tell us: "Flee also youthful lusts: but follow righteousness, faith, charity [love], peace, with them that call on the Lord out of a pure heart. But foolish and unlearned questions avoid, knowing that they do gender strifes. And the servant of the Lord must not strive."

The servant of the Lord must not be in strife. You are a servant of the Lord, so you cannot quarrel, bicker and fight with anyone, "But be gentle unto all men, apt to teach, patient, in meekness instructing those that oppose themselves [or those that are in strife and opposition to one another]; if God peradventure will give them repentance to the acknowledging of the truth; and that they may recover themselves out of the snare of the devil, who are taken captive by him at his will" (2 Timothy 2:24-26).

> *Always take the Word way. Always take the faith way. Stand immovable on the promises of God.*

You cannot afford strife. It puts you in a position to be taken captive by Satan at his will. You are no longer a civilian. You are a soldier of the Cross. You have answered the call and taken your place in the ranks of the forces of Almighty God. Put on the armor and fight the good fight of faith. If you surrender to the enemy, you will be worthless to the kingdom of God. The last thing God needs is for His army to become prisoners of war!

When you are not walking in love and have strife in your life, the gifts of the Spirit are stopped. First Corinthians 13:1-3 says:

> Though I speak with tongues of men and of angels, and have not charity [love], I am become as sounding brass, or a tinkling cymbal. And though I have the gift of prophecy, and understand all mysteries, and all knowledge; and though I have all faith, so that I could remove

mountains, and have not charity [love], I am nothing. And
though I bestow all my goods to feed the poor, and though
I give my body to be burned, and have not charity [love],
it profiteth me nothing.

The word of wisdom and word of knowledge, the gift of faith,
gifts of healing, working of miracles, discerning of spirits,
tongues, interpretation of tongues and prophecy are nine weapons
of our warfare. If Satan attacks them individually, he has nine
fights on his hands. But he can defeat them all in one stroke simply by causing strife among those who are operating in the gifts.
He then gains control legally because he is allowed to. James 3:16
says, "Where envying and strife is, there is confusion and every
evil work." It is no wonder there has been so much confusion connected with the operation of the gifts of the Spirit.

Take control of the devil by standing on the Word of God and
controlling your feelings and emotions—the place where strife is
born. To control your emotions, you must control your tongue. The
Bible says that the person who can control his words can gain mastery over his entire body (James 3:2).

Make a quality commitment to the Word of God.

Be dedicated.

Decide to please the Father.

Decide to live in victory.

Decide to walk the life of love.

Decide to live by faith.

Make the quality, no-turning-back decision that if your faith
won't get it, then you won't have it—because you are determined to live by faith. ⌘

Don't ever make the choice to do it the easy way and not believe God for it. When it comes down to it, stand on the Word and use your faith. Always take the Word way. Always take the faith way. Stand immovable on the promises of God.

Now Begin Enjoying It

Make the quality decision to have a ministry of excellence—to be a vessel of honor—yielded to God's Word to do His will in the earth. God will honor you as you honor Him. When you make the commitment of dedication to God and His Word, nothing will be able to change your stand of faith. You'll know the truth and the truth will make you free. And as you put the Word out in faith and love, those to whom you minister will be made free. You will move in the gifts of the Spirit with confidence, knowing that the weapons of your warfare are mighty through God to the pulling down of strongholds.

Tape/CD 1 Outlined

I. Demand the same excellence from yourself that you demand from God
   A. God has set the standard for us
   B. Demand excellence from the ministries involved with

II. Entrusted with God's strength and might
   A. Two responsibilities
      1. Develop and maintain excellence of ministry
      2. Deal with Satan

III. The first step to excellence in ministry is *dedication*
   A. A decision based on commitment to God
   B. Moved by what God says, not feelings
   C. Nothing can turn you from your commitment
   D. Do not go into the ministry without it
   E. Most costly thing on this planet is being out of the will of God

IV. Calling of God is without repentance
   A. Every man is responsible for his calling and will stand in judgment for it
   B. Find your calling and get in it
   C. May have to overcome wrong thinking to find your place

V. You are the deciding factor of what you will be
   A. Vessel of gold and silver to honor
      1. You are important to God
      2. Extension of His creativity; a tool of the Master Craftsman
      3. He is the vine, you are the branch

VI. Devote yourself to pleasing God
   A. Be spiritually minded
   B. Live by faith
   C. Live the love walk

VII. Purge yourself from strife or Satan will take you captive at his will
   A. Stops the gifts of the Spirit
   B. Brings confusion
   C. Stop it by controlling your feelings and emotions
      1. Control emotions by setting a watch over your mouth

VIII. Always take the Word way
   A. Stand immovable on the promises of God

Study Questions

(1) List some characteristics of a ministry of excellence._____

_____

_____

_____

(2) Define a "quality decision."_____

_____

_____

_____

(3) What must you do to become a vessel of honor?_____

_____

_____

_____

(4) How can believers be likened to the tools of a master craftsman?___

_____

_____

_____

_____

(5) How do you stay out of strife? _____

_____

_____

_____

_____

Study Notes

Study Notes

"And the servant of the Lord must not strive; but be gentle
unto all men, apt to teach, [and] patient."
2 Timothy 2:24

2

"He that wavereth is like a wave of the sea driven with the wind and tossed. For let not that man think that he shall receive any thing of the Lord. A double minded man is unstable in all his ways."

James 1:6-8

A double-minded man tries to live by faith and protects his fear all at the same time. He talks both ways out of his mouth.

TAPE/CD TWO
Singleness of Purpose

Your Singleness of Purpose Should Be to Meet the Needs of the People

"Go ye into all the world, and preach

the gospel to every creature."

Mark 16:15

Single-Minded to Do God's Will

FOCUS: "But whoso looketh into the perfect law of liberty, and continueth therein, he being not a forgetful hearer, but a doer of the work, this man shall be blessed in his deed" (James 1:25).

Mark 16:15 says, "Go ye into all the world, and preach the gospel to every creature." If Jesus said, "Go," then to you it ought to be in capital letters and you ought to go whether you feel like it or not. The Word should be the thing that moves you, not a feeling.

Jesus was moved by compassion—love. He was not moved by a *feeling* of compassion. God's Word dictated what He did. He was committed to it. He had one thing in mind: fulfilling the will of God.

Step two to excellence in ministry then is *singleness of purpose*. Our singleness of purpose is to meet the needs of the people. By doing God's will, putting His Word first place and making it final authority in everything you do, God can work through you to meet the needs of the people.

James 1:1-8 says:

> James, a servant of God and of the Lord Jesus Christ, to the twelve tribes which are scattered abroad, greeting. My brethren, count it all joy when ye fall into divers temptations; knowing this, that the trying of your faith worketh patience. But let patience have her perfect work, that ye may be perfect and entire, wanting nothing. If any of you lack wisdom, let him ask of God, that giveth to all men liberally, and upbraideth not; and it shall be given him. But let him ask in faith, nothing wavering. For he that wavereth is like a wave of the sea driven with the wind and tossed. For let not that man think that he shall receive any thing of the Lord. A double minded man is unstable in all his ways.

A double-minded man is one who hesitates. Why? He has not made a firm decision what he is going to do. He is irresolute. He is not resolved to handle things once and for all without changing his mind. A double-minded man has not really made a decision at all. He goes back and forth from one viewpoint to another. He is "unstable in all his ways" (verse 8).

What happens when you hesitate? Your adversary takes the first step. You find yourself on the defensive with Satan ahead of you, beating you at every turn. If you are not single-minded about your purpose for being in the ministry, you will not have any definite direction. You will always be wondering what you are supposed to do.

Don't Hesitate to Step Out on Your Faith

FOCUS: "Therefore, my beloved brethren, be ye stedfast, unmoveable, always abounding in the work of the Lord, forasmuch as ye know that your labour is not in vain in the Lord" (1 Corinthians 15:58).

Do you remember when you felt the first symptom of a cold or the flu strike you but you waited around for two or three days before picking up your Bible and praying about it? Then, later on you wondered why you waited until you were sick before you acted. Your hesitation gave the sickness an opportunity to get a hold on you. Hesitating is *not* a quality of a single-minded person. It is a characteristic of "a man of two minds (hesitating, dubious, irresolute)." (James 1:8, *The Amplified Bible*).

Irresolute means "indecisive." It describes a man who has not thoroughly resolved things in his mind and settled them once and for all. "...[He is] unstable and unreliable and uncertain about everything [he thinks, feels, decides]" (James 1:8, *TheAmplified Bible*).

If a man is of two minds, then the decisions he makes are split. When you get into an area of indecision, you are at a standstill. You won't go either way.

A double-minded man is one who tries to live by faith and

protects his fear at the same time. He talks both ways. His "faith" proclaims, "I believe God is going to heal you—someday." His fear whispers, *I wouldn't want to say that you are well just yet.* Inconsistency is hazardous. If you are hesitating in stepping out on your faith in ministry, your adversary will always be one step ahead of you. You will never see the power of God work through you to heal anyone.

> *Our single purpose as ministers of God is to meet the needs of the people.*

Luke 8 records an event in the life of Jesus that illustrates the danger of instability and hesitancy.

> Now it came to pass on a certain day, that he went into a ship with his disciples: and he said unto them, Let us go over unto the other side of the lake. And they launched forth. But as they sailed he fell asleep: and there came down a storm of wind on the lake; and they were filled with water, and were in jeopardy. And they came to him, and awoke him, saying, Master, master, we perish. Then he arose, and rebuked the wind and the raging of the water: and they ceased, and there was a calm. And he said unto them, Where is your faith? And they being afraid wondered, saying one to another, What manner of man is this! for he commandeth even the winds and water, and they obey him (Luke 8:22-25).

Jesus stated when they first entered the ship, "Let us go over unto the other side of the lake" (verse 22). There was enough power in those words to get the disciples all the way across the lake. Yet, they became afraid and ran to awaken Jesus crying, "Master, master, we perish" (verse 24). This is a perfect illustration of double-mindedness. They were speaking death to the author of life. They were speaking fear in the very presence of faith personified, the Son of the living God. They were consumed with the problem while the solution Himself slept in their vessel.

"We perish" didn't sound unstable to them, but to Jesus, it was a direct contradiction of what He had stated. When Jesus said to them, "Let us go over unto the other side of the lake," He *knew* without a shadow of a doubt where they were going. The disciples should have known too. They should have stood in the bow of that ship and shouted out, "The Son of the living God, the Christ, has told us to go over to the other side. Now, peace, be still!" If they were not capable of exercising such faith, Jesus would not have the right to rebuke them after He stilled the storm. "Why are ye so fearful? how is it that ye have no faith?" (Mark 4:40).

> *A single-minded man makes quality decisions and settles them forever.*

The disciples were filled with wonder and astonishment. "What manner of man is this, that even the wind and the sea obey him?" (verse 41). Jesus had just spent an entire day expounding on the power of God to these men and instructing them in what the Word would do. Then, when He demonstrated it before their eyes, they were dumbfounded. Instead of standing on the Word as He did, they were double-minded.

A single-minded man makes quality decisions and settles them forever. If you are going to put the Lord, His work and Word first in your life, there will be times when you will have to bypass what you see in order to meet the people's needs. Don't hesitate. Do whatever it takes.

Preach the Word in Season and Out

FOCUS: "For the word of God is quick, and powerful, and sharper than any twoedged sword, piercing even to the dividing asunder of soul and spirit, and of the joints and marrow, and is a discerner of the thoughts and intents of the heart" (Hebrews 4:12).

The Apostle Paul instructed young Timothy, "Preach the word;

be instant in season, out of season...., do the work of an evangelist, make full proof of thy ministry" (2 Timothy 4:2, 5).

Preach the Word. When your congregation says, "We've got financial problems," don't hesitate. Deliver the gospel. When you have a building program to complete, preach the Word. When your church says, "It can't be done," get with it. Don't spend your time trying to figure out how to get things done or how to get people to give.

If no one is giving, then you are not preaching the Word. People will support you if you feed them spiritually.

You may say, "But I have no place to preach!" Preach it on the street corner if you must, but do it! Minister to everyone you meet, everywhere you go!

Many very good, well-intentioned men have sought God's anointing by praying earnestly, "Oh, God, I've got to have Your power manifest in my ministry!" They have spent hours and days praying, interceding and fasting. Every minister wants God's power and the gifts of the Spirit to manifest through them. Some would give anything in this world if someone they laid hands on would fall out under the power of God! You can beg until you change color, but it's only when you start preaching the Word that that power begins. Your job is to meet the needs of the people. The Word of God has the answer to every need. When you deliver the Word, signs will follow.

When you roll all the care of it over on God and simply say, "Well, Lord, You want them saved more than I do. You want them healed more than I do. You want their needs met more than I do. So I'm just going to preach the Word. I'll preach it in season and out of season. I'll preach it at night. The only thing I'll ever be accused of doing too much is preaching the Word! Whether they respond or not, I'll preach the Word! I will not be swayed by anything or anybody; I will preach the Word!"

Preach it to yourself first and then to everybody you come in contact with. Be willing to walk away from *anything* in order to get God's Word to others. When you make that kind of a decision, on the authority of the written Word of God, signs will follow your ministry, the necessary funds will come in, and you will have more places to preach than you can handle.

If you have one dollar, use it to share the gospel. If you have a thousand dollars, use it to minister the Word. If you have a hundred thousand dollars, use it to fulfill your calling.

When you get through, preach some more. When you get tired, when you don't feel well, and even when you feel better, *go preach!*

God's Word is all you need. The Scriptures will save you, heal you, fill you with the Holy Spirit. They will turn you into the righteousness of God and meet your needs according to His riches in glory. The Word of God will sustain you in every way. "So then faith cometh by hearing, and hearing by the word of God" (Romans 10:17). A man filled with faith can do *anything he can believe.* All things are possible to him who believes.

> *If there is ever a choice between the Word and anything else, choose the Bible way.*

If there is ever a choice between the Word and *anything* else, choose the Bible way. If you are a musician and God uses you in music, put the gospel to music. Whatever talent God has given you, use it to preach the good news!

God sticks by the Book. When you stay with the Word, God will stay with you. The Bible says that He is "upholding all things by the word of his power" (Hebrews 1:3). If you want to be upheld, then get on His promises! ◅◐

Follow the Leadership of the Holy Spirit

FOCUS: "But the anointing which ye have received of him abideth in you, and...teacheth you of all things, and is truth, and is no lie, and even as it hath taught you, ye shall abide in him" (1 John 2:27).

In order to stay single-minded on the things of God, the third step to excellence in ministry is to *rely on the leadership of the*

Holy Spirit and not on your own understanding.

The Holy Spirit is our teacher and guide who leads us in accordance with God's will. By Him we have the mind of Christ and can handle every situation with the wisdom of God.

When ministering, never follow the path your mind wants to take. Don't lean to your own understanding. Learn to follow the leadership of the Holy Spirit within you. He is there inside you to lead you.

> *The Holy Spirit is our teacher and guide who leads us in accordance with God's will.*

When Brother Copeland first started in ministry, he had been preaching for about two years in various churches, usually ones where no one else would preach.

One day the Lord spoke to him to get out of those churches and to start holding meetings of his own. He prayed about it, and the Lord led him to Wichita Falls, Texas. He rented an old, abandoned drugstore building and some folding chairs.

One Wednesday night, the anointing was strong. He preached on the *Reality of Righteousness.* The meeting was going great, and he was having the time of his life. But just as he built the sermon to its climactic moment and God was coming forth with the finish, a woman in the audience suddenly burst forth in tongues.

He felt as if someone had stood up and doused him with a fire hose. He said, "Lady, hold that." She kept on. Again, "Lady, hold that until I finish." She got a little louder. He shouted, "In the Name of Jesus, shut up!" She grew louder still. By this time the service was in shambles. He finally just stood back and let her go on and on and on. It seemed to him that she went on for an hour and a half. Then she shifted over into English. "Yea, yea, saith the Lord...." She never said anything intelligible.

This continued for what seemed like an eternity. After a while, everyone was squirming around in their seats. They looked as if they were about ready to wring her neck. Finally, when she was quiet, Brother Copeland looked right at her and said sternly, "Well, we've already lost what we were studying anyway, so I am going to teach you something. You wouldn't have had the nerve to interrupt me in English while I was preaching, so why would you do it in a language you don't understand?"

About that time, a man sitting next to her spoke up and said, "Brother Copeland, she is stone deaf. She didn't hear a word you said."

What do you do faced with a situation like that? Whatever you say can and will be held against you. What is there to say, anyway?

Brother Copeland found out later that someone had planned the whole thing. They had already run half a dozen preachers out of town with the same trick. The woman was being used by some very selfish people. It had been arranged so that when the man next to her punched her with his elbow, it was "her turn" to prophesy.

During times like these, your decision to meet the needs of the people must rise to the surface. Jesus said that the Holy Spirit would lead you into all truth and that His sheep would know His voice. Brother Copeland was determined that no demonic spirit would run him out of town.

It was so heavy in there and so quiet. Everyone was just waiting to see what Brother Copeland would do. He closed his eyes and inside his own consciousness said, *Lord, You will have to show me what to do. I am not going to make a move until You tell me what I am to do.*

The answer came to him. It was so simple that his carnal mind would never have thought of it. He would not have even acted on it had he thought of it!

The Lord said, *Call her up and lay hands on her, and I will open her ears.* Brother Copeland said to the man next to her, "Sir, bring her up here. I am going to lay my hands on her, and God will open her ears." The man would not budge, so Brother Copeland called her to come forward and laid hands on her, and God opened her ears.

Brother Copeland finished his sermon on righteousness, and everyone had a marvelous time under the Anointing of God. The meeting grew, and that old drugstore soon filled up. Many received from God.

If you are going to minister to peoples' needs, you will have to be led of the Holy Spirit because more often than not you will find yourself in situations that only His wisdom can handle.

Some years later, Brother Copeland was preaching in Fort Worth, Texas. There were about 2,000 people in attendance one evening and unknown to him, among them was a witch who had brought a "human chalice" with her. A human chalice is a person used by witches to receive and accumulate demonic spirits. (You may encounter some of these people someday.) They attend gospel meetings for the purpose of gathering demonic spirits that are cast out of others.

To many people the idea of witches and witchcraft may seem ridiculous. However, these things do exist. We, as ministers of Jesus Christ, will have to contend with them, just as our Lord dealt with them.

The witch sat across the aisle from the chalice and was using her to create a disturbance in the meeting. Every child in the place was crying. Everyone was restless and moving about. Unless a situation like this is controlled quickly, a whole service will be ruined.

When these kinds of situations arise, you must be prepared beforehand. Unless you have spent time in prayer, you will not be able to effectively deal with these situations.

You can forget about being led by the Holy Spirit if you spend your preparation time tending to personal affairs, playing golf with influential people, making business appointments, and selling your tapes and records. Hire someone else who is anointed to handle those things. Spend your time in prayer and in the Word before a meeting. Otherwise, you will simply not be spiritually prepared to minister the Word and to overcome the obstacles that Satan will surely throw in your path. Don't ever substitute hard work for prayer.

When the disturbance arose that evening, Brother Copeland asked the Lord what to do. The Lord said, *Bind that disturbance.* Many times it will not even be necessary for you to speak aloud, just say under your breath, "In the Name of Jesus."

In this particular case (and this is why you must listen to the Spirit of God), since Brother Copeland was instructed to bind the disturbance, he said, "You spirit of disturbance, in the Name of Jesus Christ of Nazareth, I take complete and total authority over you now, and I cast you out of this place!"

Every child in that auditorium hushed. The whole audience

became quiet and still. One of the ushers spotted the chalice and came up behind her without her being aware of his presence. He heard her whispering to the evil spirit, "Come on back! Come on back!" Finally, she became so upset, she screamed, got up and ran out of the building. When that happened, the witch jumped up and ran out behind her. They fled so fast they ran into Brother Copeland's young son in the lobby and knocked him down.

At that moment Brother Copeland's mind went completely blank. He could not remember what he had been preaching. What should you do in a case like that?

Thank God, you don't have to speak out of your mind. Brother Copeland just began preaching in tongues at the direction of the Holy Spirit. The whole time 1 Corinthians 14:13 kept running through him: "Wherefore let him that speaketh in an unknown tongue pray that he may interpret."

He had not spoken in tongues long, before he changed over into English. He preached in English for about forty minutes with no idea what he was saying. At the end of that time, it was just as though he had come right back to the place he had left off.

Suddenly, he remembered the very last word he had spoken forty minutes before. He took the next word, finished the sentence, kept right on preaching and completed the sermon.

> *You must be totally grounded in and dependent on the Word of God.*

That service was one of the most anointed Brother Copeland had ever had. Later, when he listened to the recording of that service, he discovered what he had said during the forty minute interval when he had spoken solely by the Anointing of the Spirit.

To be led of God, you, as a minister, will have to be attuned to the Holy Spirit. You cannot lean to your own understanding. You must be totally grounded in and dependent on the Word of God. You must "let the word of Christ dwell in you richly in all wisdom" (Colossians 3:16).

Don't Be Influenced by Situations

FOCUS: "But none of these things move me, neither count I my life dear unto myself, so that I might finish my course with joy, and the ministry, which I have received of the Lord Jesus, to testify the gospel of the grace of God" (Acts 20:24).

On another occasion Brother Copeland was preaching in the mountains of Jamaica where sometimes, it is so dark at night you can't see the outline of your hand in front of your face. About one hundred fifty people were gathered in one small room, so jam-packed that they could hardly move. Everyone except Brother Copeland was black, and the room itself was in total darkness, except for a kerosene lantern. It was hung over his head so that he could read his Bible. All he could see was his Bible and the feet of the man right in front of him—not his face, only his feet.

The first ten or fifteen minutes were the most difficult preaching Brother Copeland had ever done. He began to realize how much he depended on the facial expressions of the audience to determine how his sermons were being received, adjusting his message or delivery accordingly. He was unaware he had been doing this.

He stopped quietly for a moment and in his own spirit said, *In the Name of Jesus, I make this firm, quality decision. For the rest of my ministry, I will never preach another sermon except by faith. I will not be swayed by the expressions of people.* He finished ministering that night and had a glorious time doing it.

Later he learned that even had he been able to see the people's expressions, he might have misinterpreted their reaction to the gospel message. They had been so influenced by British tradition and custom that they showed very little expression, if any.

If the manifestation of a miracle happened to any of them during a service, for example, it was their custom for that person to go to the pastor after the meeting and inform him privately of what had occurred. The pastor would then pass the information on to the visiting minister, if he so chose.

One lady had been completely healed of blindness during one of the meetings. She never let on that anything had taken place. It took her some time to work up the nerve to come and tell Brother Copeland about it. She was almost rigid and when she found him outside simply said, "Brother Copeland, I was blind but now I can see. Thank you." That was all. A miracle had taken place, and yet she *seemed* totally unemotional about it. So he learned another valuable lesson from this experience: Don't be influenced by emotional reactions or physical expressions of the people while you are ministering the Word. Be totally led and motivated by the Holy Spirit. ☙

> *Be led and motivated by the Holy Spirit.*

Be Prepared for Disturbances

🖋 **FOCUS:** "…On the sabbath day he entered into the synagogue, and taught…. And there was in their synagogue a man with an unclean spirit; and he cried out, saying, Let us alone; what have we to do with thee, thou Jesus of Nazareth? art thou come to destroy us? I know thee who thou art, the Holy One of God" (Mark 1:21, 23-24).

From Jamaica Brother Copeland went to Little Rock, Arkansas. There he was preaching in a place provided by the Dairyman's Association. Suddenly one evening, every light in the place went out. Then the sound system, the air conditioning, the tape recorder and everything else went completely off. It was totally dark.

Your first reaction, in the natural, might be to stop and say something like, "What happened to the lights?" Don't stop preaching regardless of what happens or what anyone else does. Never let disturbances stop you unless it is a situation in which you have to deal with people. Then, just pause long enough to find out what the Spirit of God says to do about it—but don't be caught at a loss for what to say or do. In every disturbance, the confession of your heart and mouth should be, "I am led by the Spirit of God. I am a son of God, and I am more than a conqueror in this situation."

As Brother Copeland continued, he could hear the people snickering. They didn't know what to do. Finally, the Holy Spirit said to him, *Give an invitation to receive the Holy Ghost.* He did. Three people responded. Even though he could barely see their outlines, when he laid hands on them, they all received the Holy Spirit.

When the lights came back on, he acted as if nothing had happened. Everyone else may want to acknowledge the situation, but if you don't, they will follow your lead. You are in charge of the service, so *you* be the master of it. Keep control at all times.

> *Your ministry will not be effective if you are not prepared to base it on fellowship with God.*

You should know everything that is happening in that meeting. This is the reason you must spend the hours it takes to be quiet, open your spirit to God and listen to Him. You will then be spiritually prepared for whatever happens and be able to follow the leading of the Holy Spirit.

God's principal method of guiding His people, individually and collectively, is through the ministry of His Holy Spirit—not by prophecies, dreams, visions or other "supernatural" phenomena. He may choose to speak or lead through one or more of these ways, and on occasion does. But that is not His best. Jesus said, "Howbeit when he, the Spirit of truth, is come, *he* will guide you..." (John 16:13). This is God's way of leading in our lives. To enjoy excellence in your calling, you must depend on the guidance of the Holy Spirit.

Prayer is the key. Your ministry will not be effective if you are not prepared to base it on fellowship with God. It is in your prayer time, which includes praying in the spirit, that you will find out from God what He wants you to preach and how to conduct yourself. Nothing can be substituted for prayer.

Now Begin Enjoying It

A ministry of excellence focuses on meeting the needs of the people. It is entirely motivated by the love of God. As you put the Word first place and make it final authority in everything you do, you will be moved by compassion, not feelings. When you become rooted and grounded in the Word of Love, His words will become your words and His power will begin to come out of your mouth. As a result, the needs of the people will be met and the captives will be set free.

❧ *T a p e / C D   2   O u t l i n e d* ❧

I. One area of dedication is to be obedient to the written Word of God
   A. What Jesus said should be your directive
   B. Ministry is not based on feelings
      1. Jesus moved with compassion, not a *feeling* of compassion

II. Step two to excellence of ministry is *singleness of purpose*
   A. Be single-minded on the Word
      1. A double-minded man receives nothing
         a. He hesitates
         b. He is irresolute

III. Step three to excellence of ministry is to *rely on the leadership of the Holy Spirit* and to not lean on your own understanding
   A. Several incidents that demonstrate this:
      1. Deaf woman disrupting services received her healing
      2. Witch and "human chalice" that caused disturbance left suddenly
      3. Preached in Jamaica in a place so dark he couldn't see people
         a. Woman received her sight
      4. Lights went out during a meeting, but he continued preaching as if nothing had happened
         a. Three people received the Baptism in the Holy Spirit

IV. Prayer is the key to hearing from God and following His lead
   A. Must depend on the Holy Spirit's guidance to achieve excellence

(1) What should be the motivating force in your ministry?

❧ *S t u d y   Q u e s t i o n s* ❧

_____

_____

_____

(2) Discuss step two to excellence in ministry. _____

_____

_____

_____

(3) Explain the characteristics of a double-minded man. _____

_____

_____

_____

(4) What is God's principal method of guiding His people, individually and collectively? _____

_____

_____

_____

_____

(5) What will be the result of basing your ministry on prayer and fellowship with God? _____

_____

_____

_____

_____

Study Notes

Study Notes

"*Preach the word; be instant in season, out of season.... do the work of an evangelist, make full proof of thy ministry.*"
2 Timothy 4:2, 5

3

"Trust in the Lord with all thine heart; and lean not unto thine own understanding. In all thy ways acknowledge him, and he shall direct thy paths."

Proverbs 3:5-6

If you are going to minister to people's needs, you will have to

be led of the Holy Spirit because more often than not you will

find yourself in situations that only His wisdom can handle.

TAPE/CD THREE
Separation from the World

"Sanctify them through thy truth: thy word is truth. As thou hast sent me into the world, even so have I also sent them into the world. And for their sakes I sanctify myself, that they also might be sanctified through the truth."
John 17:17-19

You Are the Righteousness of God

FOCUS: "For he hath made him to be sin for us, who knew no sin; that we might be made the righteousness of God in him" (2 Corinthians 5:21).

Just before His crucifixion, Jesus prayed a special prayer for His disciples. He said, "They are not of the world, even as I am not of the world. Sanctify them through thy truth: thy word is truth" (John 17:16-17).

To *sanctify* means "to separate unto." We are *in* this world but not *of* it. So to have excellence of ministry, we must strip away everything of the world from our lives until there is nothing left but the Word of God.

> *You must strip away everything of the world from your life until there is nothing left but the Word of God.*

One of the first things that must be rooted out is sin. You must cease confessing sin consciousness and that you and your congregation are "just old sinners saved by grace." You *were* old sinners; but since we have been saved, you are now made the righteousness of God. That *old sinner* tag is part of a sin consciousness that needs to be stripped away. "For he [God] hath made him [Jesus] to be sin for us, who knew no sin; that we might be made the righteousness of God in him" (2 Corinthians 5:21). If you do sin, activate your right-standing with God by confessing it and receiving your forgiveness (1 John 1:9). He is faithful and just to forgive and to cleanse you. Look at yourself and other believers that way. Emphasize your right-standing with God. When you minister to your congregation, teach them who they are in Christ and what a glorious inheritance they have right now because of what He has done for us.

Second, strip away your negative confessions. Don't confess that you are sinful, needy, weak or sick. Find out what God has said about you and confess the truth. You are what the Word says you are.

You are redeemed from the curse of the law. Make Galatians 3:13-14 your constant confession to yourself and to your congregation: "Christ hath redeemed us from the curse of the law, being made a curse for us...that the blessing of Abraham might come on the Gentiles through Jesus Christ."

What is the blessing of Abraham? Health, prosperity, success, wisdom, righteousness. (See Deuteronomy 28:1-14.) Confess these things!

Jesus said:

> Out of the abundance of the heart the mouth speaketh. A good man out of the good treasure of the heart bringeth forth good things: and an evil man out of the evil treasure bringeth forth evil things. But I say unto you, That every idle word that men shall speak, they shall give account thereof in the day of judgment. For by thy words thou shalt be justified, and by thy words thou shalt be condemned (Matthew 12:34-37).

Learn to control your speech. Watch out for verbal expressions and clichés like "I was scared to death." "That tickled me to death." "I could have died." Do it out of respect for Jesus. He paid for your redemption, so express yourself based on God's Word. You of all people ought to know that you can have what you say. Besides, those expressions are simply not true. You were not scared or tickled to the point of dying; you were not at all on the verge of death.

When you have grown to the point in your spiritual life where you have confidence in the integrity of your own word, you won't have any difficulty believing that God's Word is good. Then, you will eliminate those "idle words."

As a minister of the gospel, you set the example. You must make absolutely certain that what you say is true and honest. If you want God to bless what you preach, you will have to put away exaggeration and telling stories that are just not so.

Your life must be lived by faith. What you preach applies to you too. This brings the double responsibility, then, to feed the flock and to feed yourself. The Word works the same for everyone. Depend on nothing but God's Word to put you over.

Everyone has heard this type of "evangelistic talk" at one time or another. This is the same kind of "trade puffery" used by Madison Avenue in every radio and television commercial. Never be guilty of sounding like used car salesmen and carnival barkers.

Don't say there were "better'n eight hundred" in a meeting, when there were only four hundred fifty in attendance. When a handful are saved, don't say there was a "landslide of souls brought into the kingdom." A man of the Word dares not engage in such self-delusion. "For by thy words thou shalt be justified, and by thy words thou shalt be condemned" (Matthew 12:37).

Do Away With Spiritual Junk Food

FOCUS: "And be not conformed to this world: but be ye transformed by the renewing of your mind, that ye may prove what is that good, and acceptable, and perfect, will of God" (Romans 12:2).

Put the Word of God first place in your life and allow it to strip away all the other things. It won't work while you sit and watch television day and night. Break the habit.

By putting God's Word first, you are replacing priorities. Whereas before you found no satisfaction in what you did, now you have peace in your inner man. Dissatisfaction indicates your Word level is low. It has been put in second place to some natural, physical thing.

At one time Brother Copeland greatly enjoyed reading the newspaper. Through the years, it almost became an addiction. He *had* to read it every day. There is nothing wrong with watching television or reading the paper, but it is not necessary that you do so. It may be detrimental to your spiritual life.

You should be spiritually nourished every day. A steady diet of the mass media is harmful to your spiritual health and growth just as a "junk food" diet is to your physical body. You cannot "feed" on television and be a "good minister of Jesus Christ."

The media generally dwell on the negative side of life—wars, inflation, accidents, death, conflicts—and the Bible says that the cares of this world will choke the Word (Matthew 13:22). Do not allow the media to determine what you believe. You know nothing personally of those giving out the information, so do not take their word without question. Instead, put your trust in God. Rely on what He has said. He will never lie or misrepresent the truth.

In 1967, Brother Copeland made a decision to fast the newspaper for two weeks and to spend that time in the Word. He never went back to it. Occasionally, he picks one up to look through it, but the attraction is gone. The reason he lost interest is simple: He was getting more out of the Word of God than from the newspaper. It caused the separation he needed.

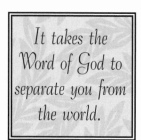

It takes the Word of God to separate you from the world.

There is nothing wrong with reading the newspaper. This is not a gospel of "don'ts." Brother Copeland merely emphasizes he receives more from the Word of God than from any of these other things in life.

In the past he derived satisfaction from things like month-long fishing trips, riding motorcycles, hunting or flying. These things were all enjoyable. But now, instead of receiving contentment *from* these things, he is satisfied *before* he does them. When your Word and confession level get low, you have a tendency to begin seeking something in the natural to satisfy that craving. It takes the Word of God to separate you from the things of this world. Unnecessary things take up your time and dilute the power of God operating in and through you.

Put Away Man-Made Schemes

FOCUS: "Trust in the Lord with all thine heart; and lean not unto thine own understanding. In all thy ways acknowledge him, and he shall direct thy paths" (Proverbs 3:5-6).

As a minister, you cannot be satisfied with being "as honest as the next fellow." You are called to be holy even as God is holy, regardless of what pressures Satan may bring to bear. You have to do "double duty" as a man of God. You must practice what you preach. Your faith and confidence must rest on the infallible Word of God and not on your own shrewd dealings.

> *Your faith and confidence must rest on the infallible Word of God and not on your own shrewd dealings.*

For example, during a series of meetings Brother Copeland held in Ruston, Louisiana, problems plagued them from the beginning. When he arrived, he learned the building he had rented in advance was a "rat trap." It smelled like rotten tennis shoes. The crowds were sparse and Brother Copeland was homesick. The devil was attacking his mind, telling him no one cared about him or his ministry. He discovered during the last meeting he was still $900 short of meeting the budget. He immediately began wondering how he was going to get the people to give.

He began to act out of fear and panic instead of by faith in the Word of God. He lost sight of the fact that God could send someone to that meeting for the specific purpose of meeting his needs. By allowing himself to become consumed with the problem, doubt and confusion took over. Had he not straightened up, he would have closed the door to what God wanted to do and given Satan the opportunity to intercept the person whom God was sending with the funds. Doubt could have cost him the victory.

In desperation Brother Copeland rationalized, "God, now I've been faithful to Your cause. My credit is good. I know what I'll do.

I can just get out of town quietly and leave the bills unpaid for just a little while. I can pay them from what I receive from the next meeting." Had he done this, it would have wrecked the next meeting's budget before he ever arrived there. That kind of reasoning leads to disaster. Once you start, your downfall is assured—it's just a matter of time.

God is everywhere. He works from both ends of a problem at the same time. Your knowledge and understanding of the situation doesn't even scratch the surface. In cases like this, the Father is trying to get you out of the way, so He can intervene. His reputation is on the line, not yours. If you will exercise faith and trust, the solution will come.

Brother Copeland became panicky. *Maybe,* he thought, *if I ran down to the newspaper office and took out a full-page ad, it would attract enough people here tonight to reach that budget."* Satan distracted him from meeting the needs of the people by getting him to think about how he could gather a big enough crowd to bring in the money.

Had he taken out an ad, it would have only added another $500 or more to the already fractured budget. He learned that his commitment to excellence kept him from leaning on his own understanding. ᴄᴏ๏

Lay Aside the Cares of This World

FOCUS: "Be careful for nothing; but in every thing by prayer and supplication with thanksgiving let your requests be made know unto God. And the peace of God, which passeth all understanding, shall keep your hearts and minds through Christ Jesus" (Philippians 4:6-7).

At the same meeting, Brother Copeland also came to understand that he had to let the Word separate him from the cares of this world. With that unmet budget staring him in the face, he got his Bible and turned to every scripture in the Word of God that guaranteed, by the blood of Jesus, his expenses were met. He looked up verses like Matthew 6:33 that says, "But seek ye first the kingdom of God, and his righteousness; and all these things [you need] shall be added unto you." and Matthew 7:7 that says, "Ask, and it shall be given you...." He read "But my God shall supply all your need according to his riches in glory by Christ Jesus" (Philippians 4:19) and "Give, and it shall be given unto you...." (Luke 6:38).

> *Let the Word separate you from the cares of this world.*

Then he went to 1 Peter 5:7: "Casting all your care upon him; for he careth for you." Brother Copeland rolled the care of the expenses over on the Lord and promised Him that with the Holy Spirit as his helper he would not touch that problem in his thought life again.

Brother Copeland prepared himself to preach and told Satan, "If you bother me anymore about this thing, I'll not even take up an offering tonight. I will get it by faith, and when I do, I'll just have added another testimony to give in my next meeting."

He wanted to worry so badly! He went into the courtyard of the motel and walked around the swimming pool. Every time he thought about the problem, he would say out loud, "No, I have rolled the care of that over on the Lord. I will not think about it. The budget is met." He kept quoting the Word of God to himself and to Satan. He had to keep talking out loud to keep his mind from worrying because he couldn't worry as long as he had to think about what he was saying.

After a while, a man drove up into the driveway and began to honk his horn. Brother Copeland saw him but didn't respond because he does not visit with people when he is in prayer or in meditation. He tried to ignore the man, but the man kept honking the horn. Finally, he stuck his head out the car window and shouted, "Come here!" It was with such authority Brother Copeland obliged the man and walked toward his car.

The man said, "Brother Copeland, I'm sorry to disturb you, but I had to get your attention. I'm committed to another obligation and will be late for the meeting tonight. I was afraid I would miss the offering." The man handed him a check. Brother Copeland prayed over the gift, shook the man's hand, then went back to his room and opened it. The check was for $500! The offering in the service that night was for the exact amount he needed for the remainder of the budget expenses.

Brother Copeland paid all the bills and left town knowing full well that the Word works. Had he not rid himself of the care and cast it over on God, the need would probably have never been met.

There is only one way you will get to the place where people will chase you down to put money into your offering. And that is for you to put the Word of God first place and make it final authority. Strip away everything else but the Word!

Now Begin Enjoying It

When you refuse to compromise or to tolerate unbelief within your ministry, you will make no provision for failure. Walking with and listening to the Holy Spirit will ensure your ability to handle anything the devil throws your way. The Holy Spirit will always lead you in accordance with the Word, so your victory is assured. As you continue to become righteousness-of-God minded, the old sin consciousness will be stripped away and you will be able to minister with the assurance that comes from knowing who you are in Him.

Tape/CD 3 Outlined

I. Excellent ministry refuses to compromise and tolerate unbelief
   A. Tolerate people but set them free in love

II. God uses apostles, prophets, evangelists, pastors and teachers to teach the Church
   A. What they say is the same as if God were talking to you
   B. High Priest

III. The fourth step to excellence in ministry is to *separate yourself from the world*
   A. The Word separates you
      1. Strip away a sin consciousness
      2. Stop talking unbelief
      3. Put your trust in God and not media reports

IV. The world offers no inner satisfaction but the Word gives peace

V. The Word works the same way for everyone
   A. Preach living by faith
   B. Practice living by faith

Study Questions

(1) Define the word *sanctify* and explain how to accomplish this in your life. _____

_____

_____

_____

(2) How do you develop confidence in the integrity of God's Word?

_____

_____

_____

(3) Identify symptoms that would indicate your confession and Word level are getting low. _____

_____

_____

_____

(4) Explain how to let the Word separate you from the cares of this world._____

_____

_____

_____

(5) What is the double responsibility of a minister? _____

_____

_____

_____

Study Notes

Study Notes

"Let the word of Christ dwell in you richly in all wisdom; teaching and admonishing one another in psalms and hymns and spiritual songs, singing with grace in your hearts to the Lord."

Colossians 3:16

4

"This book of the law shall not depart out of thy mouth; but thou shalt meditate therein day and night, that thou mayest observe to do according to all that is written therein: for then thou shalt make thy way prosperous, and then thou shalt have good success."

Joshua 1:8

A ministry of excellence is a ministry

that does not plan to fail.

> ## TAPE/CD FOUR
> ### Look to the Word
> ### Day and Night

"My son, attend to my words;
incline thine ear unto my
sayings. Let them not depart
from thine eyes; keep them in
the midst of thine heart."
Proverbs 4:20-21

When the going gets tough, the pressure builds, and it

seems like everybody in the world and all hell put

together are arrayed against you, God demands that

you walk by the Word and by nothing else.

Look to the Word Day and Night

FOCUS: "O how love I thy law! it is my meditation all the day" (Psalm 119:97).

A ministry of excellence does not plan to fail. When you minister to someone, keep your faith applied no matter what it looks like in the natural. That person has come to you to receive his need met, so approach the situation in a positive, victorious manner. Should you close the service and there is still no outward manifestation of what you believed for, it does not mean you failed. The Word never fails and if you preached the Word, it is still at work.

As you continue to look to the Word it will produce several effects on your ministry that you cannot get any other way. You will obtain God's favor, increase your faith and your understanding of how to use your faith. Luke 11:49 refers to the Word of God as His wisdom. Proverbs 4:5-9 reads:

> Get wisdom, get understanding: forget it not; neither decline from the words of my mouth. Forsake her not, and she shall preserve thee: love her, and she shall keep thee. Wisdom is the principal thing; therefore get wisdom: and with all thy getting get understanding. Exalt her, and she shall promote thee: she shall bring thee to honour, when thou dost embrace her. She shall give to thine head an ornament of grace: a crown of glory shall she deliver to thee.

The ornament of grace Solomon referred to is being clothed with the favor of God. It is the result of seeking God's wisdom by exalting His Word, which in turn, brings divine favor. The wisdom of God places a crown of glory (God's grace or favor) upon your head. This grace, or favor, is available to every person on earth

The wisdom of God is His written Word.

without exception, for "God is no respecter of persons" (Acts 10:34). Favor cannot be earned. It is the gift of God. You do not merit it; you receive it. Although it is free, God's grace is not automatic. It must be appropriated by the believer through faith.

We already know that "faith cometh by hearing, and hearing by the word of God" (Romans 10:17). The basis for receiving God's favor is through faith. Therefore, you obtain God's favor through His Word.

God created the heavens and the earth through a combination of His faith, wisdom and understanding (Proverbs 3:19; Hebrews 11:3). In Mark 11:22, Jesus exhorts His disciples, "Have faith in God." The marginal note in the *King James Version* reads, "Have the faith of God." Another version puts it this way: "Have the God-kind of faith." The faith that is in you is exactly the same faith that is in God. He gave you the same measure of faith (Romans 12:3).

If God could create the entire universe with His faith, then why are believers so limited in their ability to bring things to pass using that same force? Why is God so much more successful? Because He has the wisdom and understanding to use it to its fullest capacity.

Wisdom is the ability to use knowledge. First Corinthians 1:30 says that Christ Jesus is made unto us wisdom. He is your wisdom. "We have the mind of Christ" (1 Corinthians 2:16).

Whenever you think of God's wisdom or knowledge, you are thinking of the Word of God. God said:

> For my thoughts are not your thoughts, neither are your ways my ways, saith the Lord. For as the heavens are higher than the earth, so are my ways higher than your ways, and my thoughts than your thoughts.... So shall my word be that goeth forth out of my mouth: it shall not return unto me void, but it shall accomplish that which I please, and it shall prosper in the thing whereto I sent it (Isaiah 55:8-9, 11).

In other words God is saying, "Even though I think higher than you think and My ways are higher than your ways, I give you My Word so you will be able to think like I do and conform to My ways."

The wisdom of God is His written Word. He shares His knowledge with you through the Word as evidenced by 2 Corinthians 10:5, "Casting down imaginations, and every high thing that exalteth itself against the knowledge of God, and bringing into captivity every thought to the obedience of Christ." Jesus Christ is the Word (John 1:14). If Jesus Himself is the Word and if He is made unto you wisdom, then you can conclude that true wisdom is the Word of God. God and His Word agree at all times. With these thoughts in mind, you could rephrase Proverbs 4:5-9 in this way:

> Get [the Word]: forget it not; neither decline from the words of my mouth. Forsake [the Word of God] not, and [it] shall preserve thee: love [the Word], and [it] shall keep thee. [The Word] is the principal thing; therefore get [the Word]: and with all thy getting get understanding. Exalt [the Word], and [it] shall promote thee; [it] shall bring thee to honour, when thou dost embrace [it]. [It] shall give to thine head an ornament of grace: a crown of glory shall [the Word] deliver to thee.

Remember: Look to the Word day and night. Proverbs 4:20-22 says, "My son, attend to my words; incline thine ear unto my sayings. Let them not depart from thine eyes; keep them in the midst of thine heart. For they are life unto those that find them, and health to all their flesh."

Exalt the Word. Let it do the work. If there is ever a problem, apply God's wisdom to it. Speak and act only on the Word. If you exalt the Word, people will be delivered. ✑

The Word Promotes

FOCUS: "Wisdom is the principal thing; therefore get wisdom: and with all thy getting get understanding. Exalt her, and she shall promote thee: she shall bring thee to honour, when thou dost embrace her. She shall give to thine head an ornament of grace: a crown of glory shall she deliver to thee" (Proverbs 4:7-9).

If you will refrain from exalting yourself but instead lift up the Word of God, then it will promote you and bring you to a place of honor. Peter tells us, "Humble yourselves therefore under the mighty hand of God, that he may exalt you in due time: casting all your care upon him; for he careth for you" (1 Peter 5:6-7).

Humble yourself by placing yourself in God's hands and casting the whole of your care upon Him. Hold your tongue. Don't pull strings to gain position or vie for power—you might get it. If you wrangle it on your own, then you will have to produce on your own without any help from the Spirit of God. If He didn't place you in a position of honor, He will not sustain you there. You will be responsible for your own failures.

> *Exalt the Word to such a degree that God receives all the credit for what is accomplished in your ministry.*

You should exalt the Word to such a degree that in every instance God receives all the credit for whatever is accomplished in your ministry. For example, suppose someone in your congregation should stand up and testify, "I just want to praise the Lord for that car wreck that put me in the hospital because one night I cried out to Him. If it hadn't been for that car wreck, I would have never gotten right with God."

Don't let that kind of testimony go uncorrected in your church. In love and kindness teach your people not to give credit to disasters for restoring them to God. God's Word will make you right with God—not sickness or disease. It was not the wreck that spoke to that person, sustained him and revealed God to him. The wreck did not restore him to health. It was God's Word that produced all these things. The promises were there before the wreck, during his hospital stay and after his release. Don't give glory to an automobile wreck, to a sickness or disease, or to any other catastrophe or tragedy. Give the credit to the Word of God for being strong and the upholding power even in the midst of Satan's attacks. In doing so, you are magnifying God.

During your church services if there is ever any doubt about which direction the service is headed, lead it toward the Word. If you are short on time, cut out everything except the Word. Put the Word first. If you do this, all the other things will take care of themselves.

Jesus said, "But seek ye first the kingdom of God, and his righteousness; and all these [other] things shall be added unto you" (Matthew 6:33). In order to put the Word first, you will have to feed on it night and day. You must program your mind with it and get rid of all the other rubbish that has been fed into your consciousness. Satan will see to it that it will not be an easy task. To overcome him, you need an intensive, total immersion in the Word, night and day—not just a casual reading of the Scriptures for a few minutes.

A music major in college practices for hours every day. Olympic skaters spend six to eight hours daily training for their routines. We, as ministers, ought to discipline ourselves in the Word twenty-four hours a day—especially in the beginning years.

This may well mean you will have to take your messages of successful, uncompromising ministers of the Word around with you everywhere you go. Permeate your mind with the New Testament and solid, Bible-based sermons. Do whatever it takes to become totally saturated with the Word. It may mean that you will have your razor in one hand and your media player in the other, or your media player in one hand and a fork in the other. You may have a media player in the car, in your lunch bag, and on the nightstand. You might even use a media player for an alarm clock! This is meditation on the Word day and night.

You may say, "I can't do that all the time." Then you'd better think twice about the ministry. If you are not willing, you would be wise just to find some undemanding bureaucratic position in some denominational hierarchy, sit behind a desk and push a pencil. There is nothing wrong with that kind of work or those who fill those positions, but it must be stressed that if you have made a definitive decision to amount to something in the ministry of Jesus Christ and are determined to take the Great Commission seriously, then you must be diligent. You must be prepared to do battle.

A commanding officer would speak no differently if he were sending you into combat against the best-trained, elite troops of a savage enemy. If you ever find yourself untrained, untaught and suddenly thrust into battle against Satan's storm troopers, you will understand the gravity of the situation. You are God's frontline assault force. Don't let yourself be deceived about what you are about to confront.

You have an enemy who is doing his level best to destroy you. You will be fired upon. If you should be wounded, don't expect to be graciously nursed back to health by sympathetic supporters behind the lines. In carnal warfare, the wounded are awarded Purple Hearts and are treated as heroes. In the war against Satan, the wounded are often torn to shreds by their own people. If you fall as a minister, not only will your "loyal" church members not give you a medal, they will probably dishonorably discharge you from service and send you back to selling shoes.

While Brother Copeland was in the service, he asked his sergeant in basic training, "Why are you being so hard on us? Why do we have to train this hard? I can understand the necessity for thorough training, but you are the meanest thing on two feet." He looked him straight in the eye and growled, "I'm going to tell you something, boy. When I come walking down the road someplace in the midst of an invasion and find some man lying in the ditch with his guts blown out, it's not going to be my fault!"

Like any good soldier, to survive the war, you must take your training seriously. If you will do these things, you are guaranteed success as a member of God's handpicked storm troopers in these last climactic days.

In this crucial, all-out, no-holds-barred offensive, Satan has dispatched hell's choicest personnel to annihilate you and to assure that you never open your mouth to preach the gospel again. He is merciless. He will do everything in his power to destroy everything you have and everything you touch. That is why when the going gets tough, the pressure builds, and it seems like everybody in the world and all hell put together is arrayed against you, God demands that you walk by the Word and nothing else. You will have to go the Word way when it seems like nothing is working. God's integrity can take the pressure. Just hold tight to the Word. ᴄᴏ

Looking to the Word Helps Control Your Flesh

FOCUS: "Thy word have I hid in mine heart, that I might not sin against thee" (Psalm 119:11).

When Kenneth and Gloria Copeland first started in the ministry, Brother Copeland became more and more aware of God's demand to spend all of his time in the Word—not part of the time, not the majority of it, but all of it. They carried a tape recorder loaded with gospel material everywhere they went. It played all the time.

At that time, they had two small children and were constantly traveling. They preached on the average, twenty-one days each month, twice a day. For a long time they did not take a vacation.

Together, they set up the meetings. Brother Copeland ran the tape recorder and the sound system. Gloria Copeland helped with the meetings and took care of the children. After the services, they both sold tapes. They did it all without any help.

After the last meeting, Brother Copeland would excuse himself, go change clothes and dismantle the equipment. All this can be done when the Word of God is going in and out of your consciousness at all times.

After about two years of this, Brother Copeland became so Word oriented that he automatically judged everything he heard or experienced by the Word. The Bible became his standard. He retrained himself until the Bible way became habitual.

Hebrews 5:12-14 describes it this way:

For when for the time ye ought to be teachers, ye have

need that one teach you again which be the first principles of the oracles of God; and are become such as have
need of milk, and not of strong meat. For every one that
useth milk is unskilful in the word of righteousness: for
he is a babe. But strong meat belongeth to them that are
of full age, even those who by reason of use [habit or
practice] have their senses exercised [trained] to discern
both good and evil.

By staying in the Word, Brother Copeland's senses learned to
discern between good and evil. His body and mind became so
trained that even his flesh rejected evil.

People have the mistaken idea that you have to fight against
carnality until Jesus comes to free the Body of Christ. This is not
true. You must simply walk in the spirit. The body has no nature of
its own. It will do whatever it is told. People have said, "The nature
of God is in your spirit, but the Adamic nature is in your body."
That nature was not Adamic in origin, it was satanic.

In the first place, sin was never Adam's nature. Adam had the
nature of God. Adam's original nature was perfection. Satan's nature
took root in him and caused the problem. Adam invited that nature
through high treason, but it wasn't in his body. It was in his spirit.
His body was trained to follow his spirit.

Your body will do whatever it is trained to do. If your reborn
human spirit dominates your flesh, all of your actions will be godly
ones. This can be proven. Let your body stand up or sit down right
now without your command. It cannot. It is trained to follow
instructions. God created the body in such a way that it could be
trained to follow instructions. Your physical body is trained to such
a degree that it will function automatically without conscious
direction. A well-programmed machine without a nature of its
own, your flesh operates totally at your command and for your
benefit. You eat, walk, talk, drive and go through a thousand other
daily activities with little or no conscious thought. But you had to
learn to do all these things at one time or another. You have been
trained to do them, and your body responds automatically.

At the Fall, Satan took advantage of the fabulous way that God
intended the human system to work. He introduced doubt, fear and

every other evil thing imaginable until he had programmed man's carnal mind to sin and death.

Man can sin without even thinking about it. Most people have become so proficient at sinning they don't even need to try; it comes quite "naturally"! Their bodies have been trained to do it.

How then can you ever hope to overcome this situation? The answer is found in Romans 12:1-2, "...present your bodies a living sacrifice, holy, acceptable unto God, which is your reasonable service. And be not conformed to this world: but be ye transformed by the renewing of your mind, that ye may prove what is that good, and acceptable, and perfect, will of God."

Present your body as a sacrifice to God. Reprogram yourself to automatically act on the Word. Your body will be retrained.

By continuing to put the Word of God into your mind, spirit and body, you will eventually come to the place where the Word controls all three. Then the Spirit becomes the dominant force in your life and everything else conforms to it. You will have become separated from the world and will have become Word controlled. ᘓ

God will exalt you as you exalt the Word. Everything will start "coming your way" because of that Word. And as it comes, give it away. "Give, and it shall be given unto you" (Luke 6:38). In this way, you will not only be blessed, you will become a channel of God's blessings to others. If you are to be a minister in the truest and fullest sense, you must look to the Word day and night.

Now Begin Enjoying It

When you put the Word first place, it will prosper and promote you. It never fails. When you preach it, it is still at work regardless of appearances. So as you humble yourself, casting the whole of your care on Him and exalt His Word, people will be delivered and you will become a channel of His blessings to others.

❧ *T a p e / C D   4   O u t l i n e d* ❧

   I. A ministry of excellence does not plan to fail
     A. Approach every situation in a positive, victorious manner

  II. Step five to excellence in ministry is *look to the Word day and night*
     A. The written Word is God's wisdom
       1. See Proverbs 4:5-9
       2. Will give you an ornament of grace

 III. The Word will exalt you
     A. Humble yourself under God
       1. Cast *all* your care
         a. Have the God-kind of faith

 IV. Reprogram your mind to think in line with God
     A. Listen to anointed messages from successful, uncompromising ministers of the Word
     B. Listen to recordings of the Bible

  V. Looking to the Word day and night will help you control your flesh
     A. Senses trained to discern between good and evil
     B. Present your body as a sacrifice to God
       1. Reprogram yourself to automatically act on the Word

 VI. God will exalt you as you exalt the Word
     A. Everything will start "coming your way"
     B. Give it away

❧ S t u d y   Q u e s t i o n s ❧

(1) A ministry of excellence is one that does not plan to fail. Explain. _____

_____

_____

_____

(2) What is the fifth step to excellence in ministry? _____

_____

_____

_____

(3) What is God's wisdom?_____

_____

_____

_____

(4) How do you "look to the word day and night"? _____

_____

_____

_____

(5) Explain how looking to the Word will help you control your flesh._____

_____

_____

_____

_____

Study Notes

Study Notes

"*So then faith cometh by hearing, and hearing by the word of God.*"
Romans 10:17

5

"And Jehoshaphat...set himself to seek the Lord, and proclaimed a fast throughout all Judah."

2 Chronicles 20:3

Fasting was not given to us to make God do

something. You don't have to make God do

anything that is to your advantage. He's already

paid for your advantage.

TAPE/CD FIVE
Take Time to Fast

"Then I proclaimed a fast there, at the river of Ahava, that we might afflict ourselves before our God, to seek of him a right way for us, and for our little ones, and for all our substance."
(Ezra 8:21)

Fasting Brings Areas to the Surface That Need Correction

So You Can Deal With Them in the Light of the Word

When You Fast

FOCUS: "But thou, when thou fastest, anoint thine head, and wash thy face; that thou appear not unto men to fast..." (Matthew 6:17-18).

There are two general types of fasts. One type, a proclaimed fast, is one that is declared. For example, a pastor announces that he is calling his entire congregation to voluntarily refrain from food for a certain length of time. The purpose of the fast varies. Most often it is for a time of special prayer.

Another example of a proclaimed fast is a husband and wife who agree to refrain from marital relations for a specific period of time to give themselves to prayer and fasting. Paul speaks of this in 1 Corinthians 7:5, "Defraud ye not one the other, except it be with consent for a time, that ye may give yourselves to fasting and prayer; and come together again, that Satan tempt you not for your incontinency." This is a proclaimed fast, a time of mutual consent where both you and your spouse may fast at the same time.

Second Chronicles 20 records a proclaimed fast and its results. During the reign of Jehoshaphat, king of Judah, word was brought to him that a vast army was marching toward Jerusalem to attack his nation. "And Jehoshaphat feared, and set himself to seek the Lord, and proclaimed a fast throughout all Judah. And Judah gathered themselves together, to ask help of the Lord: even out of all the cities of Judah they came to seek the Lord" (2 Chronicles 20:3-4).

The people were called together into the temple and a fast was declared. They determined not to eat until they heard from the Lord. Jehoshaphat prayed, leaning on the promises of protection and deliverance God had made to Abraham and his descendants. In answer to his supplication, the Spirit of God spoke through a Levite and gave them instructions. By following the directions, the victory was theirs. A proclaimed fast will put you in the position to hear from God to receive guidance for a specific situation.

The other general type of fast is a personal fast, one that is not announced to anyone. It only involves you and God.

Always consider your family. The other members of the

household may not want to go on a fast with you. Arrangements should be made for their meals, especially if you are the one who prepares them. God will give you the grace to cook the meals for the others without being bothered by it if it's done in love. This is done so strife will not enter in. Strife will destroy the results of the fast.

Here are some guidelines: Jesus said, "Moreover when [not if—fasting is not optional] ye fast, be not, as the hypocrites, of a sad countenance: for they disfigure their faces, that they may appear unto men to fast. Verily I say unto you, They have their reward" (Matthew 6:16).

Hypocritical piety will defeat the purpose of a fast. If you publicize your spirituality, you will exchange the reward of God for a reward of men. Their esteem becomes the only recompense you will receive for the effort.

"But thou, when thou fastest, anoint thine head, and wash thy face; that thou appear not unto men to fast, but unto thy Father which is in secret: and thy Father, which seeth in secret, shall reward thee openly" (Matthew 6:17-18).

> *fasting will keep you keen to the voice of God for guidance.*

This passage of scripture is part of the Sermon on the Mount. Jesus was not primarily teaching on fasting but rather about hypocrisy and pretension. He spoke of giving alms, praying publicly on street corners and fasting. He gave examples of how men ought to worship God in humility, not making a show of their good deeds.

We are not to make our fasting conspicuous. We should dress, groom and conduct ourselves in a normal fashion so we do not call attention to what we are doing.

The purpose of fasting is not to influence God into acting in our behalf. Abstaining from food does not impress Him. Its purpose is to shut off the influence of our flesh in order to be in tune with the Spirit. It brings areas to the surface that need correction so you can deal with them in the light of the Word. It will keep you keen to the voice of God for guidance in your life or the lives of others for whom you are interceding.

Be careful not to fast in order to receive visions or apparitions from the Lord. Brother Copeland made that mistake, and God sternly reprimanded him for it. He showed him that Satan would love to step in and manifest himself as an angel of light to deceive him (2 Corinthians 11:14). He made a quality decision not to seek visions. Although, if the Father wants to give them to you, that is fine. But determine to base your faith and receive revelation only through the Word of God.

Brother Copeland knew a man who supernaturally received revelation about the authority of the believer some years ago. He wanted more, but rather than go to the written Word of God, he decided that Jesus would have to appear to him in person.

He set himself to fast until Jesus appeared to him. Not having eaten for more than forty days, he nearly died. Jesus did come and speak to him, but later, Brother Copeland heard him relate what Jesus had told him. He could have found every bit of it in the book of Ephesians. The man already had a word from the Lord in print. But from then on, every time he had the least problem he went right back to the same maneuver. Over a period of time, he became totally dependent on fasting to receive a vision to know God's will. He departed more and more from the Word of God. Before long he was receiving things that were not from God. He was in so much error that after a while his ministry lost its credibility.

Anything you receive aside from the Word of God will not produce faith. Faith comes by hearing and hearing by the Word of God (Romans 10:17). When trials and tribulations come, if your faith is based on the written Word, you then have a strong foundation. When you receive revelations or visions, you have a source from which to compare spiritual things with spiritual. The Word is a more sure word of prophecy than the voice of God from heaven (2 Peter 1:18-20).

Fasting helps you to receive from God but does not push God to action. You don't have to do anything to move God to exercise His power for you. He has already paid dearly for that privilege. The problem is not God's unwillingness to help you nor His inability to intervene on your behalf. The problem is the believers' spiritual density, the inability to receive what God has already done at Calvary. Fasting is a tool that puts you in position to be more spiritually aware and "tuned in" to God so you can better receive from Him. ✑

Rewards of Fasting

FOCUS: "But thou, when thou fastest...thy Father, which seeth in secret, shall reward thee openly" (Matthew 6:17-18).

"Shall reward thee openly" is an outright statement of promise right from the lips of Jesus Christ. When you fast, you have a reward coming.

What would that reward be? It is certainly not a pat on the back for not eating. The reward is whatever motivated you to fast. Whatever it is, establish it by faith and proclaim it before you ever enter the fast. Expect to receive it. God will see in secret and you will receive openly.

When you fast, you have a reward coming.

Perhaps you fast for no other reason than to fellowship with God. That is a sound reason, and you will receive your reward of divine fellowship.

It may be to understand something from the Word that you know God has been trying to reveal to you, but you haven't been able to grasp. That should be the reward you seek in your fast.

Perhaps you have been praying for unsaved family members. You may feel that there should be more you can do to see them saved. Your fast may be undertaken as a time of special intercession.

In this case, you are not trying to motivate God to save them. He has been trying to do that for years. You are simply making a faith connection with the Father, giving Him the opportunity and the faith to get that job accomplished. Establish that as your reward.

This is also true of a proclaimed fast. Declare the purpose of the fast and that will be the reward.

The Fast God Has Chosen

FOCUS: "And I set my face unto the Lord God, to seek by prayer and supplications, with fasting…" (Daniel 9:3).

Isaiah 58:6-7 deals with fasting, observance of the Lord's ordinances and the keeping of His Sabbath. In this chapter the Lord says, "Is not this the fast that I have chosen? to loose the bands of wickedness, to undo the heavy burdens, and to let the oppressed go free, and that ye break every yoke? Is it [God's chosen fast] not to deal thy bread to the hungry, and that thou bring the poor that are cast out to thy house?"

Why would God tell you to take the food you would have eaten had you not fasted and given it away? You would do this to get the attention of the poor—to bring the poor to your house. For what purpose? To witness to them about the Lord Jesus Christ.

Satisfy their physical hunger first, then feed them spiritually. Through the new birth and the power of the gospel, you can teach them how to be delivered from poverty. "When thou seest the naked, that thou cover him; and that thou hide not thyself from thine own flesh?" (verse 7).

God is referring to fasting something more than food. He is talking about fasting clothes. You can do without some clothes as well as without food so you can give to someone who has less than you. Consciously put yourself in the position of giving to others.

Verse 8 says, "Then shall thy light break forth as the morning, and thine health shall spring forth speedily: and thy righteousness shall go before thee."

What does righteousness have to do with it? Jesus said, "But seek ye first the kingdom of God, and his righteousness; and all these things shall be added unto you" (Matthew 6:33). Anything you give away will begin to come back to you.

Don't give away rummage and junk. Give your good things away. "For with the same measure that ye mete withal it shall be measured to you again" (Luke 6:38). "For whatsoever a man soweth, that shall he also reap" (Galatians 6:7). What you give will determine what you receive. If you give your junk, you will receive junk!

Isaiah 58:8 continues: "And thy righteousness shall go before thee; the glory of the Lord shall be thy rearward." The word "rearward" literally means "rear guard" or "rear protection." As we obey the fast God has chosen, we can take the offensive and know that God is on the defensive in our behalf.

Verse 9 says: "Then shalt thou call, and the Lord shall answer; thou shalt cry, and he shall say, Here I am. If thou take away from the midst of thee the yoke, the putting forth of the finger, and speaking vanity."

A requirement for the success of the fast God has chosen is to stop judging and accusing others. That kind of talk is all vain. Let your words always be with grace.

"And if thou draw out thy soul to the hungry, and satisfy the afflicted soul; then shall thy light rise in obscurity, and thy darkness be as the noon day: And the Lord shall guide thee continually, and satisfy thy soul in drought, and make fat thy bones: and thou shalt be like a watered garden, and like a spring of water, whose waters fail not" (verses 10-11).

As you are obedient to these scriptures, you will experience an abundance of God's guidance for your life and ministry. You will be fulfilled. The rivers of living water Jesus spoke of will quench your spiritual thirst, and you will have plenty for others to draw on from you.

Look at verses 12-13:

> And they that shall be of thee shall build the old waste places: thou shalt raise up the foundations of many generations; and thou shalt be called, The repairer of the breach, The restorer of paths to dwell in. If thou turn away thy foot from the sabbath, from doing thy pleasure on my holy day; and call the sabbath a delight, the holy of the Lord, honourable; and shalt honour him, not doing thine own ways, nor finding thine own pleasure, nor speaking thine own words.

The Sabbath day was the established day of fasting for Israel. God has not bound us to a certain day in which we are commanded to fast, but He has instructed us in the way we should conduct ourselves when we do. Put pleasures aside. Meditate on these verses, and consider what God commanded to be done on His day. Many have missed its true significance. The day of the week is not as important as we have thought. God is much more concerned about how His people conduct themselves.

"Then shalt thou delight thyself in the Lord; and I will cause thee to ride upon the high places of the earth, and feed thee with the heritage of Jacob thy father: for the mouth of the Lord hath spoken it" (verse 14). (This is also the promise Brother Copeland stood on to receive the first airplane he needed for the ministry.)

What is the "heritage of Jacob" which we are to receive through fasting? To answer that question, refer back to Deuteronomy 32:9-14:

> For the Lord's portion is his people; Jacob is the lot of his inheritance. He found him in a desert land, and in the waste howling wilderness; he led him about, he instructed him, he kept him as the apple of his eye. As an eagle stirreth up her nest, fluttereth over her young, spreadeth abroad her wings, taketh them, beareth them on her wings: So the Lord alone did lead him, and there was no strange god with him. He made him ride on the high places of the earth, that he might eat the increase of the fields; and he made him to suck honey out of the rock, and oil out of the flinty rock; butter of kine, and milk of sheep, with fat of lambs, and rams of the breed of Bashan, and goats, with the fat of kidneys of wheat; and thou didst drink the pure blood of the grape.

The heritage of Jacob insures that you hear the voice of the Good Shepherd and are not led astray by the evil one. It guarantees your provision of oil for fuel—it takes gasoline to preach the gospel!

You are also promised prosperity and abundance in the middle of financial depression. Those things have already been provided in Christ. Fasting merely puts you in a better position to receive them because you are not letting your flesh dominate you. When you truly put God first in every area of your life, then you license Him to be your provider of all things.

These verses reveal what Jesus meant when He spoke in Matthew 6 about the reward. If done properly, fasting can be beneficial physically, circumstantially and spiritually. Reap the full benefits of fasting and see the difference it can make in your personal life, as well as in your ministry.

For quick reference, here is a summary of the proper way to fast:

(1) Decide the purpose of the fast before you begin.

(2) Proclaim the fast before the Lord. Whether proclaimed or personal, it must be declared before God, or you will be tempted to break it. This must be a decision of quality. Say, "Father, with You as my Helper, in the Name of Jesus, I have settled this today, and until this time tomorrow food will not pass my lips." Once you have made that firm commitment, you will stick by it.

(3) Believe before the fast that you receive the reward promised by Jesus in Matthew 6:18. Actually, this assurance is based on Mark 11:24: "What things soever ye desire, when ye pray, believe that ye receive them, and ye shall have them." You are not going to receive because you fast. You will receive because you believed in faith. Fasting is an assistance to receiving.

(4) Minister to the Lord while you are fasting. Ministering to the Lord in praise and worship will keep your spirit active and build you up. You will need the additional strength to bear up (Colossians 3:16; Ephesians 6:19; Acts 13:1-3).

(5) Minister to others during and after the fast. During your fast minister to others only as God leads you to do so. Always be available. But remember, fasting is a period of preparing yourself for greater ministry later on.

After the fast, do not think, *Well, I'm never going to fast again. I didn't receive a thing from God during the whole time I was on the fast.* Yes, you did. Now, minister to other people, and you will find out that you have received. You will witness that the power of God is great upon you.

(6) Expect assistance from the angels. After fasting forty days Jesus was confronted by Satan. After He had successfully resisted Satan's temptation, Matthew 4:11 says, "Then the devil leaveth him, and, behold, angels came and ministered unto him." The angels ministered to Jesus, and you can expect help from ministering servants, too, by faith. Don't feel for it. The worst thing you can do is go by your feelings. All they will tell you is, "I'm hungry!" Shut off your feelings. Act on your faith. Confess that the angels are attending you. Continue to thank God for it. They are licensed not only to assist you where you are but also to work for you throughout the world, wherever your influence is needed. ∽⅋

Now Begin Enjoying It

When you do these things according to God's Word, you will see and reap the results of it for years to come. You will think that you must surely be the most blessed person in the world. Things will come to you for which you have not even prayed nor asked God for. This has happened to Brother Copeland and God told him later that these things came to him because he had exalted Him months before. God was working in Brother Copeland's behalf, and he was then reaping the fruit of the seed he had sown.

❧ Tape/CD 5 Outlined ❧

I. Fasting helps promote excellence in ministry
   A. Puts you in position to be more spiritually attuned to God

II. One area of fasting is a proclaimed fast (2 Chronicles 20:3-4)
   A. Pastor calls everyone to fast
   B. Head of household or family

III. Another area of fasting is the personal fast
   A. Involves only you and God
   B. Consider others for whom you are responsible
       1. Stay out of strife
       2. Stay away from hypocritical piety

IV. Fasting assists in receiving from God
   A. Jesus promised reward
       1. Purpose of the fast is the reward
       2. Believe you receive the reward

V. The fast God has chosen
   A. Give the food or of yourself to others
       1. Satisfy their physical hunger, then spiritual hunger

Study Questions

(1) What is the reason for fasting? _____

_____

_____

_____

(2) Explain the two types of fasts. _____

_____

_____

_____

(3) Why is it unwise to rely on fasting for revelation knowledge?

_____

_____

_____

_____

(4) What is the reward of a fast? _____

_____

_____

_____

(5) What is the heritage of Jacob? _____

_____

_____

_____

_____

Study Notes

"Sanctify ye a fast, call a solemn assembly, gather the elders and all the inhabitants of the land into the house of the Lord your God, and cry unto the Lord."
(Joel 1:14)

6

Exalt the Word. Let the Word do the work. If there's ever a problem, apply the Word. Act on the Word. Speak on the Word. Do everything you do on the Word of God.

"Give me understanding, and I shall keep thy law; yea,

I shall observe it with my whole heart." Psalm 119:34

TAPE/CD SIX
Total Dedication

"My son, attend to my words....
For they are life unto those that
find them.... Put away from thee
a froward mouth, and perverse
lips put far from thee."
Proverbs 4:20-24

Make Yourself Available to God

FOCUS: "And thou shalt love the Lord thy God with all thine heart, and with all thy soul, and with all thy might. And these words, which I command thee this day, shall be in thine heart: and thou shalt…talk of them when thou sittest in thine house, and when thou walkest by the way, and when thou liest down, and when thou risest up" (Deuteronomy 6:5-7).

Brother Copeland opened this final session at Rhema Bible Training Center in Broken Arrow, Okla., to questions from the ministerial students.

First, he was asked how he got speaking engagements when beginning in full-time ministry.

Brother Copeland was attending Oral Roberts University and had been hired to help pilot Oral Roberts' airplane. At this time Oral Roberts was still traveling and holding weeklong crusades. During those meetings Brother Copeland got involved in every part of the ministry he could. He was ministering in the invalid room and praying for people night and day. When back on campus, he ministered to the students and staff who came to him for prayer. He made himself available to God twenty-four hours a day.

> *Make yourself available to God twenty-four hours a day.*

Eventually Brother Copeland began sensing God wanted him in his own ministry. He and Gloria prayed at the breakfast table one day, over an open Bible, looking up scriptures, believing God together. They joined hands and set themselves in agreement, committing their ministry to God on several levels. First, he and Gloria agreed to never ask anyone for a place to preach. Even if God told Brother Copeland He wanted him to preach at a certain place, he would make himself available but never manipulate his way in.

Second, he and Gloria agreed they would never preach on the

basis of a financial arrangement—through their initiation or someone else's. They would never preach anywhere because they had bills to pay. The ministry would not be used for gain.

While they were praying, the phone rang. A pastor in Fort Worth, Texas, was calling to ask if Brother Copeland would preach at his church. Although he knew who the pastor was, he had only attended his church a couple of times. Brother Copeland's ministry was not known at that time and the pastor had never heard him preach, but he said, "I believe the Lord wants you to come preach in my church…." Brother Copeland agreed. He went and has been busy ever since.

When you commit yourself so strictly and honestly to God that He can trust you with the power of the Word of God coming out of your mouth, you will have all the speaking engagements you can handle.

The Lord told Brother Copeland not to be dependent on a denomination, but only on the Word. The best thing you can possibly do is throw yourself completely over on the Word of God and let God make arrangements for you. When it looks as if it's not going to work out, take your stand and say, "I'm not going to do it any other way." The situation will turn.

> *Throw yourself completely over on the Word of God.*

Another student asked Brother Copeland what to do when your spouse threatens to withdraw their love if you go into the ministry.

Brother Copeland advised the minister to do nothing in reaction to that situation but to go on and preach the Word. Allow the spouse to do what they want to do. Roll the care of it over on God.

The worst response would be to attempt to persuade the spouse not to leave or to give in to them and not do what God said. This is what Adam did. Instead of doing what God told him to do, he went along with Eve and gave in to her.

So the minister must be obedient to God and stay out of strife in that situation. Since that environment is not healthy to stay around, it would be wise to treat it long distance until the other person gets over it or it is somehow resolved.

Another student asked how much time Brother Copeland spent in prayer each day. He answered that when you stay in the Word the majority of the time and your mind is constantly focused on it, you find yourself remaining in an attitude of prayer and fellowship with God. You get into an area of constantly listening to God, praying and interceding.

Brother Copeland was asked to comment on statements made by Rhema graduates now in ministry, that the future graduates would find themselves spending less time in prayer and the Word than they would like because of ministerial duties. Brother Copeland commented that when you want the Word of God and the Anointing of God as badly as you want breath, you'll make time for it. You will separate yourself and see to it that you have time for the Word of God and prayer. If you ever let anyone steal it from you, Satan will steal your ministry. When the people realize how dedicated you are to the Word of God, they'll leave you alone and even help you stay in the place of prayer and study because the results will be seen by the whole church. If you stay on the Word you will hear the voice of the Spirit and be able to take care of every situation in balance. Your time will be handled supernaturally if you put the Word and prayer first. If you put the work first, you'll never have time for the Word.

> *When you want the Word of God and the Anointing as badly as you want breath, you'll make time for it.*

When people begin receiving from God, it will draw them. They will come from every denomination and background, from every walk of life. You will grow and have more to do than you have time for.

Brother Copeland was also asked how much time he and Gloria spent in prayer together. He answered that they only spent whatever time was necessary to set themselves in agreement over things that needed prayer. They took one day at a time, dealing with whatever came up each day, rolling the care of it over on the Lord and continuing on. Since they work together, pray together and love God together—it doesn't take much time to get in agreement over what is needed.

The next question dealt with the issue of hospitality, mentioned in 1 Timothy 3:2. Many people show hospitality to keep people thinking well of them. But it can be used to be in harmony with others so that their faith will work when they need you. *The Amplified Bible* amplifies the word *hospitality* as "showing love for and being a friend to the believer."

The final question concerned hiring and paying people in your ministry. Brother Copeland said he never hired anyone unless he was impressed of God or the Lord told him to hire them. He related that when Jerry Savelle came to work for him, the ministry did not have the money to pay him. But God told Brother Copeland to bring him in to work for the ministry. Jerry did not have any of the skills Brother Copeland needed. But he was willing to learn and became so dedicated to the Word, that he prayed himself into the ability to do everything he was called on to do and even prayed in the money for his own pay.

When the Lord sends you someone and they accept the responsibility, you must commit to God to allow the person the opportunity to fail as well as to succeed. Make sure the person understands the responsibility God has given you and what their part of that responsibility is, and then get out of their way. If you try to keep your hand in it, God will not let it grow any further because you won't let any of it go. You will end up choking it. It is better to leave it alone. 〜◎〜

Conclusion:
Formula for Success

These six steps to excellence in ministry were revealed to Brother Copeland from God's Word. They will be a blessing to you as you minister the gospel of Jesus Christ. Brother Copeland has personally proven their value and validity over the years in his own ministry.

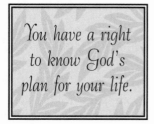

You have a right to know God's plan for your life.

The following three-step formula for success in applying these principles to your life and ministry was given to Brother Copeland years ago by a great man of God. They have been tested and proven many times over. If you will apply these truths seriously, you will have success in every area of your life. Nothing can hold it back from you. Every Christian endeavor, no matter what it is, will succeed when it is backed with this kind of prayer and dedication because God Himself is behind it.

(1) Find the will of God in your situation by prayer and meditation in the Word. You have a right to know God's plan for your life. God's Word is His will. While you are seeking God's will, ask questions of others if you must. Whatever may be involved, find God's plan for your life.

(2) Once you have determined what the will of God is, confer no more with flesh and blood. Don't seek any more advice. Don't hesitate. Just look to the Word and stand firm on it.

(3) Get your job done at all costs. If God has called you to do it, then with God you can do it. You are capable of doing anything the Word says you can do. You are what the Word says you are. Therefore, you can get the job

done no matter what the cost. You may find yourself
many times in a position where it will look so much eas-
ier to follow anything but the Word. Don't do it! Put
God's Word first place in your life and allow it to be final
authority. You will have success. All of heaven's
resources—Almighty God, Jesus of Nazareth, the Holy
Spirit, all the host of heaven—and everything in the
Bible promise that you will get your job done! And God
will be glorified in you!

Now Begin Enjoying It

The Word of God is the answer to every situation and question
in life. When you commit yourself to a ministry of excellence,
walk in close communion with the Father and put His Word first
place, He will be able to trust you with the anointing. You will hear
His voice with clarity and be able to minister His love to meet the
needs of the people.

"Now the God of peace, that brought again from the dead our
Lord Jesus, that great shepherd of the sheep, through the blood of
the everlasting covenant, make you perfect in every good work to
do his will, working in you that which is wellpleasing in his sight,
through Jesus Christ; to whom be glory for ever and ever. Amen"
(Hebrews 13:20-21)

✎ *T a p e / C D   6   O u t l i n e d* ✎

I. Question and answer session at Rhema Bible Training Center
  A. How did you get speaking engagements?
    1. Made self available to God
    2. Committed on several different levels
    3. Never preached on basis of finances
    4. Believed God—calls came
  B. What if you spouse is not in agreement?
    1. Do what God says
    2. Roll the care on Him
  C. How much time do you spend in prayer each day?
    1. Constant time and focus in the Word puts you in a place of continual communion with God
  D. Comment on having less time for prayer and Word study because of ministerial duties
    1. When you want the Word of God and Anointing of God as much as breath, you'll make time for it
    2. Separate yourself and see to it that you make time for the Word of God and prayer
    3. If you let anyone steal Word and prayer from you, Satan will steal your ministry
  E. How much time Brother Copeland and Gloria spend in prayer together?
    1. Whatever time necessary to set themselves in agreement over things needing prayer
    2. Take one day at a time
    3. Roll the care over on God
  F. What is meant in 1 Timothy 3:2 by showing hospitality?
    1. To be in harmony with others so their faith will work
    2. *The Amplified Bible* "showing love for and being a friend to the believers"
  G. Hiring and paying people in your ministry
    1. Be led of the Lord on whom to hire
    2. Once person accepts responsibility, allow them to succeed or fail
    3. Allow them to do job without interference

✎ S t u d y   Q u e s t i o n s ✎

(1) How did Brother Copeland make himself available to God?

_____

_____

_____

(2) Why is it important to totally commit yourself and your ministry to what God has called you to do? _____

_____

_____

_____

(3) Explain why it is vital not to preach based on finances. ___

_____

_____

_____

(4) Explain why you must put God's Word and prayer first place in your life and ministry. _____

_____

_____

_____

(5) What are the three steps for success in applying the principles of excellence to your life and ministry? _____

_____

_____

_____

Study Notes

Study Notes

"*The anointing which ye have received of him abideth in you....*"
(1 John 2:27)

Prayer for Salvation and Baptism in the Holy Spirit

Heavenly Father, I come to You in the Name of Jesus. Your Word says, "Whosoever shall call on the name of the Lord shall be saved" (Acts 2:21). I am calling on You. I pray and ask Jesus to come into my heart and be Lord over my life according to Romans 10:9-10: "If thou shalt confess with thy mouth the Lord Jesus, and shalt believe in thine heart that God hath raised him from the dead, thou shalt be saved. For with the heart man believeth unto righteousness; and with the mouth confession is made unto salvation." I do that now. I confess that Jesus is Lord, and I believe in my heart that God raised Him from the dead.

I am now reborn! I am a Christian—a child of Almighty God! I am saved! You also said in Your Word, "If ye then, being evil, know how to give good gifts unto your children: HOW MUCH MORE shall your heavenly Father give the Holy Spirit to them that ask him?" (Luke 11:13). I'm also asking You to fill me with the Holy Spirit. Holy Spirit, rise up within me as I praise God. I fully expect to speak with other tongues as You give me the utterance (Acts 2:4). In Jesus' Name. Amen!

Begin to praise God for filling you with the Holy Spirit. Speak those words and syllables you receive—not in your own language, but the language given to you by the Holy Spirit. You have to use your own voice. God will not force you to speak. Don't be concerned with how it sounds. It is a heavenly language!

Continue with the blessing God has given you and pray in the spirit every day.

You are a born-again, Spirit-filled believer. You'll never be the same!

Find a good church that boldly preaches God's Word and obeys it. Become a part of a church family who will love and care for you as you love and care for them.

We need to be connected to each other. It increases our strength in God. It's God's plan for us.

Make it a habit to watch the *Believer's Voice of Victory* television broadcast and become a doer of the Word, who is blessed in his doing (James 1:22-25).

About the Author

Kenneth Copeland is co-founder and president of Kenneth Copeland Ministries in Fort Worth, Texas, and best-selling author of books that include *Managing God's Mutual Funds—Yours and His, How to Discipline Your Flesh* and *Honor—Walking in Honesty, Truth and Integrity.*

Now in his 37th year as a minister of the gospel of Christ and teacher of God's Word, Kenneth is the recording artist of such award-winning albums as his Grammy-nominated *Only the Redeemed, In His Presence, He Is Jehovah* and his most recently released *Just a Closer Walk.* He also co-stars as the character Wichita Slim in the children's adventure videos *The Gunslinger, Covenant Rider* and the movie *The Treasure of Eagle Mountain,* and as Daniel Lyon in the *Commander Kellie and the Superkids*_{SM} videos *Armor of Light* and *Judgment: The Trial of Commander Kellie.*

With the help of offices and staff in the United States, Canada, England, Australia, South Africa and Ukraine, Kenneth is fulfilling his vision to boldly preach the uncompromised Word of God from the top of this world, to the bottom, and all the way around. His ministry reaches millions of people worldwide through daily and Sunday TV broadcasts, magazines, teaching audios and videos, conventions and campaigns, and the World Wide Web.

Learn more about
Kenneth Copeland Ministries by
visiting our Web site at **www.kcm.org**

Books Available From Kenneth Copeland Ministries

by Kenneth Copeland

* A Ceremony of Marriage
  A Matter of Choice
  Covenant of Blood
  Faith and Patience—The Power Twins
* Freedom From Fear
  Giving and Receiving
  Honor—Walking in Honesty, Truth and Integrity
  How to Conquer Strife
  How to Discipline Your Flesh
  How to Receive Communion
  In Love There Is No Fear
  Know Your Enemy
  Living at the End of Time—A Time of Supernatural Increase
  Love Never Fails
  Managing God's Mutual Funds—Yours and His
  Mercy—The Divine Rescue of the Human Race
* Now Are We in Christ Jesus
  One Nation Under God (gift book with CD enclosed)
* Our Covenant With God
  Partnership, Sharing the Vision—Sharing the Grace
* Prayer—Your Foundation for Success
* Prosperity: The Choice Is Yours
  Rumors of War
* Sensitivity of Heart
* Six Steps to Excellence in Ministry
* Sorrow Not! Winning Over Grief and Sorrow
* The Decision Is Yours
* The Force of Faith
* The Force of Righteousness
  The Image of God in You
* The Laws of Prosperity
* The Mercy of God (available in Spanish only)
  The Outpouring of the Spirit—The Result of Prayer
* The Power of the Tongue

*Available in Spanish

The Power to Be Forever Free
* The Winning Attitude
Turn Your Hurts Into Harvests
Walking in the Realm of the Miraculous
* Welcome to the Family
* You Are Healed!
Your Right-Standing With God

by Gloria Copeland

* And Jesus Healed Them All
Are You Listening?
Are You Ready?
Be a Vessel of Honor
Build Your Financial Foundation
Fight On!
Go With the Flow
God's Prescription for Divine Health
God's Success Formula
God's Will for You
God's Will for Your Healing
God's Will Is Prosperity
* God's Will Is the Holy Spirit
* Harvest of Health
Hidden Treasures
Living Contact
Living in Heaven's Blessings Now
Looking for a Receiver
* Love—The Secret to Your Success
No Deposit—No Return
Pleasing the Father
Pressing In—It's Worth It All
Shine On!
The Grace That Makes Us Holy
The Power to Live a New Life
The Protection of Angels
There Is No High Like the Most High
The Secret Place of God's Protection (gift book with CD enclosed)
The Unbeatable Spirit of Faith
This Same Jesus
To Know Him
* Walk in the Spirit (available in Spanish only)

Walk With God
Well Worth the Wait
Words That Heal (gift book with CD enclosed)
Your Promise of Protection—The Power of the 91st Psalm

Books Co-Authored by Kenneth and Gloria Copeland

Family Promises
Healing Promises
Prosperity Promises
Protection Promises

* From Faith to Faith—A Daily Guide to Victory
From Faith to Faith—A Perpetual Calendar

One Word From God Can Change Your Life

One Word From God Series:
• One Word From God Can Change Your Destiny
• One Word From God Can Change Your Family
• One Word From God Can Change Your Finances
• One Word From God Can Change Your Formula for Success
• One Word From God Can Change Your Health
• One Word From God Can Change Your Nation
• One Word From God Can Change Your Prayer Life
• One Word From God Can Change Your Relationships

Load Up—A Youth Devotional
Over the Edge—A Youth Devotional
Pursuit of His Presence—A Daily Devotional
Pursuit of His Presence—A Perpetual Calendar

Other Books Published by KCP

The First 30 Years—A Journey of Faith
  The story of the lives of Kenneth and Gloria Copeland
Real People. Real Needs. Real Victories.
  A book of testimonies to encourage your faith
John G. Lake—His Life, His Sermons, His Boldness of Faith
The Holiest of All by Andrew Murray
The New Testament in Modern Speech by Richard Francis Weymouth
The Rabbi From Burbank by Rabbi Isidor Zwirn and Bob Owen
Unchained by Mac Gober

*Available in Spanish

Products Designed for Today's Children and Youth

And Jesus Healed Them All (confession book and CD gift package)
Baby Praise Board Book
Baby Praise Christmas Board Book
Noah's Ark Coloring Book
The Best of *Shout!* Adventure Comics
The *Shout!* Giant Flip Coloring Book
The *Shout!* Joke Book
The *Shout!* Super-Activity Book
Wichita Slim's Campfire Stories

*Commander Kellie and the Superkids*_{SM} **Books:**

The SWORD Adventure Book
*Commander Kellie and the Superkids*_{SM} Solve-It-Yourself Mysteries

*Commander Kellie and the Superkids*_{SM} Adventure Series:
Middle Grade Novels by Christopher P.N. Maselli:

#1 The Mysterious Presence
#2 The Quest for the Second Half
#3 Escape From Jungle Island
#4 In Pursuit of the Enemy
#5 Caged Rivalry
#6 Mystery of the Missing Junk
#7 Out of Breath
#8 The Year Mashela Stole Christmas

World Offices of Kenneth Copeland Ministries

For more information about KCM and a free
catalog, please write the office nearest you:

Kenneth Copeland Ministries
Fort Worth, Texas 76192-0001

Kenneth Copeland
Locked Bag 2600
Mansfield Delivery Centre
QUEENSLAND 4122
AUSTRALIA

Kenneth Copeland
Post Office Box 15
BATH
BA1 3XN
U.K.

Kenneth Copeland
Private Bag X 909
FONTAINEBLEAU
2032
REPUBLIC OF
SOUTH AFRICA

Kenneth Copeland
Post Office Box 378
Surrey, B.C.
V3T 5B6
CANADA

Kenneth Copeland Ministries
Post Office Box 84
L'VIV 79000
UKRAINE

We're Here for You!

Believer's Voice of Victory **Television Broadcast**

Join Kenneth and Gloria Copeland and the *Believer's Voice of Victory* broadcasts Monday through Friday and on Sunday each week, and learn how faith in God's Word can take your life from ordinary to extraordinary. This teaching from God's Word is designed to get you where you want to be—*on top!*

You can catch the *Believer's Voice of Victory* broadcast on your local, cable or satellite channels.

Check your local listings for times and stations in your area.

Believer's Voice of Victory **Magazine**

Enjoy inspired teaching and encouragement from Kenneth and Gloria Copeland and guest ministers each month in the *Believer's Voice of Victory* magazine. Also included are real-life testimonies of God's miraculous power and divine intervention in the lives of people just like you!

It's more than just a magazine—it's a ministry.

To receive a FREE subscription to *Believer's Voice of Victory,*
write to:

Kenneth Copeland Ministries
Fort Worth, Texas 76192-0001

Or call:
1-800-600-7395
(7 a.m.-5 p.m. CT)

Or visit our Web site at:
www.kcm.org

If you are writing from outside the U.S., please contact the KCM
office nearest you. Addresses for all Kenneth Copeland Ministries
offices are listed on the previous pages.